ANSWERS TO COMMON QUESTIONS ABOUT

The Bible

Titles in the Answers to Common Questions Series

Answers to Common Questions About Angels & Demons
by H. Wayne House and Timothy J. Demy

Answers to Common Questions About God
by H. Wayne House and Timothy J. Demy

Answers to Common Questions About Heaven & Eternity
by Timothy J. Demy and Thomas Ice

Answers to Common Questions About Jesus
by H. Wayne House and Timothy J. Demy

Answers to Common Questions About the Bible
by H. Wayne House and Timothy J. Demy

Answers to Common Questions About the End Times
by Timothy J. Demy and Thomas Ice

ANSWERS TO COMMON QUESTIONS ABOUT

The Bible

H. Wayne House
Timothy J. Demy

Kregel
Publications

ISBN 978-0-8254-2655-1

Printed in the United States of America

14 15 16 17 18 / 5 4 3 2 1

From Wayne:
To Carrie House and Nathan House

From Tim:
To Glen Riddle,
lover of words and the Word,
books and the Book

Contents

Part 9: The Interpretation of the Bible   136

Part 10: Contemporary Challenges Regarding the Bible   142

About This Series

The Answers to Common Questions series is designed to provide readers a brief summary and overview of individual topics and issues in Christian theology. For quick reference and ease in studying, the works are written in a question and answer format. The questions follow a logical progression so that those reading straight through a work will receive a greater appreciation for the topic and the issues involved. The volumes are thorough, though not exhaustive, and can be used as a set or as single-volume studies. Each volume is fully documented and contains a bibliography for further reading for those who want to pursue the subject in greater detail.

The study of theology and the many issues within Christianity is an exciting and rewarding endeavor. For two thousand years, Christians have proclaimed the gospel of Jesus Christ and sought to accurately define and defend the doctrines of their faith as recorded in the Bible. In 2 Timothy 2:15, Christians are exhorted: "Be diligent to present yourself approved to God as a workman who does not need to be ashamed, accurately handling the word of truth." The goal of these books is to help you in your diligence and accuracy as you study God's Word and its influence in history and thought through the centuries.

Introduction

The Bible is the most important book in the history of the world. It has been studied, memorized, and burned. Politicians, pundits, and preachers routinely quote it. It has brought consolation to the weak and weary, insight to the pious and perplexed, and consolation to the distraught and dying. It is unique in its character, its content, its composition, and its influence. It has influenced individuals, groups, movements, and Western civilization far beyond what we can fully comprehend. Its influence on literature in the West is unsurpassed. A person who doesn't have some biblical literacy will be hard-pressed to understand Melville, Milton, or a host of other influential authors.

The Bible has been the best best-seller of all ages. It has been translated, paraphrased, visualized, and amplified. If you walk into any major bookstore and look at the display of Bibles, you will likely find one for any and every age group, and for readers desiring devotional Bibles, study Bibles, or theme Bibles. There are more than a dozen major translations in English (some more accurate than others), and you can find excellent Bibles on the Internet as well (e.g., the NET Bible).

The history of how we got the Bible, and of its subsequent transmission and publication, is an amazing story that fills many volumes. Not every language spoken in the world today has a corresponding Bible translation, but for the majority of people in the world, the Bible is available in their language—and each translation has a unique history. Some people have argued that the Bible is filled with codes and that its history is full of conspiracies. We don't believe that. But we do believe that the content and history of the Bible are unlike any other book ever written. Join us as we look at some of the many questions that are frequently asked about the history of the Bible as a religious and literary text. It is an amazing subject!

PART 1

The Origin of the Bible

1. When was the Bible written?

The Bible was written over the course of approximately 1,500 years (between 1440 B.C. and A.D. 100).[1] The period covered by biblical history is about 6,000 years, from the creation of Adam in the garden of Eden through the visions of St. John on the island of Patmos in the Aegean Sea at the end of the first century A.D. The recording of the people and events that precede and follow the Exodus of the Israelites, when Israel's history begins, was penned by the lawgiver-prophet-deliverer, Moses, in the fifteenth century B.C. between approximately 1440–1405 (or in the late to middle thirteenth century, according to some scholars), as the Israelites wandered in the desert of the Sinai Peninsula after leaving Egypt. Moses wrote almost the entire first five books of the Bible during this time, with someone else, such as Joshua, composing the last chapter of the book of Deuteronomy. The remainder of the Hebrew Bible (also called the Tanak by the Jews) was written over the next several hundred years by various prophets, kings, and other inspired persons and was finally completed around 400 B.C.

The dates of several Old Testament books are uncertain; they do not bear the names of their authors and sometimes record events far prior to the writing, so that the authors are not contemporary with those events. Moreover, scholars have little information about some books, such as Job, so that their authors and dates remain unknown.

Authorship and Dating of Old Testament Books[2]		
Book	**Author**	**Approximate Date Written**
Genesis	Moses	1445–1440 B.C.
Exodus	Moses	1440–1405 B.C.
Leviticus	Moses	1440–1405 B.C.
Numbers	Moses	1440–1405 B.C.
Deuteronomy	Moses (and possibly chapter 31 by Joshua)	1405 B.C.
Joshua	Joshua	1390 B.C.
Judges	Samuel?	1050–1020 B.C.
Ruth	Unknown	1020 B.C.
1 Samuel	Samuel?	1050–960 B.C.
2 Samuel	Samuel?	1050–960 B.C.
1 Kings	Jeremiah?	550 B.C.
2 Kings	Jeremiah?	550 B.C.
1 Chronicles	Ezra?	450–400 B.C.
2 Chronicles	Ezra?	450–400 B.C.
Ezra	Ezra	450–444 B.C.
Nehemiah	Nehemiah	450–444 B.C.
Esther	Unknown	470–465 B.C.
Job	Unknown	Unknown
Psalms	David, with specific psalms written by sons of Korah, Asaph, Heman, Ethan, Hezekiah, Solomon, and Moses	Primarily 1000 to 450–400 B.C.
Proverbs	Solomon and others	950–700 B.C.
Ecclesiastes	Solomon	935 B.C.
Song of Solomon	Solomon	971–931 B.C.
Isaiah	Isaiah	740–680 B.C.

Jeremiah	Jeremiah	627–585 B.C.
Lamentations	Jeremiah	586/85 B.C.
Ezekiel	Ezekiel	593–571 B.C.
Daniel	Daniel	537 B.C.
Hosea	Hosea	710 B.C.
Joel	Joel	835 B.C.
Amos	Amos	755 B.C.
Obadiah	Obadiah	841 B.C. or 586 B.C.
Jonah	Jonah	770–750 B.C.
Micah	Micah	700 B.C.
Nahum	Nahum	663–612 B.C.
Habakkuk	Habakkuk	606–604 B.C.
Zephaniah	Zephaniah	625 B.C.
Haggai	Haggai	520 B.C.
Zechariah	Zechariah	520–518 B.C.
Malachi	Malachi	450–400 B.C.

The New Testament writings record events that transpired from 6–4 B.C. (the birth of Jesus the Messiah) through the end of the first century A.D., with John's writing of the Revelation of Jesus. Unlike many of the books of the Hebrew Scriptures, the authors and dates of the New Testament are easier to assign because the persons, events, and dates are in close proximity within a period of approximately sixty years, and the confirmation of these persons and dates occurs at the end of the first century by disciples of the apostles or those who associated with these disciples.

Those who organized the New Testament placed the Gospels in the order they believed them to have been written. Two of the gospel writers, Matthew and John, were disciples of the Lord. Mark was an associate of Peter and probably his secretary, recording Peter's recollection (cf. 2 Peter 1:15). Luke never encountered the Lord or experienced the events he recorded, but he is known as a careful researcher, interviewing eyewitnesses of the actual events, conversations, and addresses he writes in his gospel. With this information in view, we see that three of the Gospels—Matthew, Mark, and Luke—were written between A.D. 50–70, while John's unique material (98 percent different) was written in the mid-80s.

The Acts of the Apostles is the only dedicated historical survey in the New Testament, largely focusing on the ministries of Peter and Paul but also explaining the beginning and growth of Christianity as it reached from Jerusalem to Rome. It was written after the completion of the three missionary journeys of Paul and ends with his first imprisonment in Rome, which occurred between A.D. 60–62. The letters of the apostles (other than John), apostolic associates, and half-brothers of the Lord Jesus are written from the late 40s. They begin with the letters of James, brother of the Lord and leader of the Jerusalem church, and with Paul's letter to the Galatian Christians; and they end with the writing of the anonymous treatise of Hebrews sometime in the 60s before the destruction of Jerusalem in A.D. 70. The apostle John wrote the remainder of the New Testament in the 80s and 90s. Alongside his gospel in the mid-80s, John also wrote three letters; and approximately ten years later, sometime in the 90s, he penned the Apocalypse (meaning "Revelation").

Authorship and Dating of New Testament Books		
Book	**Author**	**Approximate Date Written**
Matthew	Matthew	A.D. 50–60
Mark	Mark (for Peter)	A.D. 60
Luke	Luke	A.D. 58–60
John	John	A.D. 85–90
Acts	Luke	A.D. 61–62
Romans	Paul	A.D. 56/57 OR 58*
1 Corinthians	Paul	Spring A.D. 56
2 Corinthians	Paul	Fall A.D. 56
Galatians	Paul	A.D. 48 or Fall A.D. 49

Ephesians	Paul	A.D. 60
Philippians	Paul	A.D. 61 or Spring A.D. 62*
Colossians	Paul	A.D. 60 or Fall A.D. 61*
1 Thessalonians	Paul	A.D. 51
2 Thessalonians	Paul	A.D. 51
1 Timothy	Paul	Fall A.D. 62
2 Timothy	Paul	Fall A.D. 67
Titus	Paul	A.D. 64 or Summer A.D. 66*
Philemon	Paul	A.D. 60 or Fall A.D. 61*
Hebrews	Unknown	A.D. 64–68
James	James the brother of Jesus	A.D. 45–50
1 Peter	Peter	A.D. 63–67
2 Peter	Peter	A.D. 63–67
1 John	John	A.D. 90
2 John	John	A.D. 90
3 John	John	A.D. 90
Jude	Jude the brother of Jesus	A.D. 60s or 70s
Revelation	John	A.D. 90s

* Dates followed by an asterisk (*) are based on the calculations of New Testament scholar and author Harold W. Hoehner. A complete chronology of his calculations of the apostolic age can be found in H. Wayne House, *Chronological and Background Charts of the New Testament,* 2nd ed. (Grand Rapids: Zondervan, 2009), 129–32.

The Bible is a marvelous work written by forty authors on three continents in three languages, using various forms of literature, over a period of 1,500 years—all the while maintaining a consistent message of a monotheistic God who has revealed Himself and His plan for the human race.

2. Who wrote the Bible?

The Bible is the joint effort of prophets and apostles of God and God Himself. The Bible has forty human authors, including farmers, shepherds, kings, prophets, and fishermen among others.

Regardless of their background, those who wrote the Hebrew and Greek Scriptures were literate men. We have witness in the New Testament that Paul and Luke wrote Scripture. Peter identifies letters from Paul as being among the Scriptures (2 Peter 3:15–16), and Paul quotes a statement by Luke (either from his book or possibly an oral statement) as Scripture (cf. Luke 10:7 with 1 Tim. 5:18).

Most important is that God wrote the Bible through these human agents. The apostle Paul said that the Scripture (written word of God) is breathed out by God (2 Tim. 3:16), and Peter says that men of God spoke from God as they were moved by the Holy Spirit (2 Peter 1:21).

3. Where were the biblical books written and to whom were they written?

Prophets of God largely wrote the books of the Old Testament within the country of Israel to its resident Israelites. Books such as Joshua, Judges, Ruth, Samuel, Kings, Chronicles, Psalms, Proverbs, Ecclesiastes, and Song of Solomon were written to the kingdom of Israel before it split into the northern and southern kingdoms.

Before the Babylonian captivity, the prophets wrote to either the northern or the southern kingdom. For example, Hosea, Amos, and Isaiah wrote to the northern kingdom, whereas Jeremiah, Joel, Micah, Habakkuk, Zephaniah, Haggai, Obadiah, Nahum, and Zechariah wrote to Judah, the southern kingdom. Hosea wrote to both the northern and southern kingdoms, though predominantly to the north; and Jonah wrote to both kingdoms regarding Nineveh.

Ezekiel and Daniel wrote to the captives in Babylon. The books of Ezra, Nehemiah, Malachi, and Chronicles are postexilic and so were written to the restored kingdom of Israel after the beginning of the Persian conquest. We are uncertain as to the destination of books like Job.

The New Testament books were written from a variety of places by a number of different people. Matthew probably wrote his gospel from Antioch of Syria to the important church residing there.

John Mark wrote Peter's recollection of the gospel, possibly to the Christians in Alexandria. Luke, while he was with Paul in Israel, collected the information in his gospel from eyewitnesses of the words and events in the life of Jesus. Luke's gospel and its sequel, the Acts of the Apostles, were addressed to a noble Gentile by the name of Theophilus.

Paul's epistles were sent to a number of churches or individuals: Romans to the Christians at Rome; 1 and 2 Corinthians to the church at Corinth; Galatians to the Roman province in Galatia (southern Asia Minor); Ephesians to the church at Ephesus, though it may have been a circular letter to several churches in southwestern Asia Minor; Philippians to the church at Philippi (Macedonia); Colossians to the church at Colossae in Asia Minor (near Laodicea and Hierapolis); 1 and 2 Thessalonians to the church at Thessalonica. Paul wrote 1 and 2 Timothy to the pastor of the church at Ephesus; Titus to the pastor of the church in Crete; and Philemon to a slave owner who lived in Colossae.

Hebrews was written to the church in either Rome or Jerusalem, determined by the author's reference of "those from Italy greet you" (Heb. 13:24), which could refer to either. James, possibly the earlier New Testament book, addressed the Jewish Christians of the Diaspora. The letters 1 and 2 Peter went to Christians in the northern regions of Asia Minor. As for the letters of John, 1 John was written to a general Christian audience, possibly Asia Minor; 2 John was probably to either a local church or a woman in Asia Minor; and 3 John was to a Gentile believer, probably in Asia. Jude was written to unidentified Jewish Christians in a Gentile area; and Revelation was written to seven churches in southwestern Asia Minor.

4. In what languages was the Bible written?

Three languages were used by the human authors of the biblical text: Hebrew and Aramaic in the Old Testament, and Greek in the New Testament. Though like any language, these have changed through the centuries, each is still spoken, written, and read by contemporary users. Greek is spoken in Cyprus and Greece, and Hebrew is the national language of Israel. Dialects of Aramaic are spoken in small areas of Turkey, Syria, Israel, Iraq, and Azerbaijan.

The geographic regions and societies of the ancient Near East of the Old Testament, and of the eastern Mediterranean of the New Testament, were rich in linguistic history. The books of the Bible, written over the course of more than 1,400 years, reflect that heritage. The world of the Old Testament encompassed languages such as Akkadian, Aramaic, Egyptian, Hebrew, Sumerian, and Ugaritic. Centuries later, the world of the New Testament included Aramaic, Greek, Sahidic Coptic, and Latin.

Hebrew

Most of the Old Testament was written in Hebrew, the language of the Israelites (usually designated as either classical Hebrew or biblical Hebrew as opposed to later forms). The Hebrew alphabet has twenty-two letters (these can be seen in the acrostic Psalms such as Psalms 25 and 119). In 2 Kings 18:26–28 and Nehemiah 13:24, the language is called "the language of Judah," and in Isaiah 19:18, it is called "the language of Canaan." The Hebrew of the Old Testament as we know it covers the period of the first millennium B.C. and is a dialect of the earlier Old Canaanite. Since Moses lived before this time, it is sometimes asked what language he used in writing. Proto-Semitic inscriptions have been found that date to 1800 B.C. or earlier, so it is not implausible that Moses, who lived about 400 years later, could have used something similar to write the first five books of the Bible.[3]

Two different scripts of biblical Hebrew were used during the centuries in which the Old Testament books were written. The earlier script is known as paleo-Hebrew, and the later script is called Square script or Assyrian script.[4] Over the centuries, the Square script was adopted as Hebrew was written and read, but during the four hundred years of the intertestamental period between the era of the Old Testament and the era of the New Testament, Aramaic became the daily language of the Jews.

Aramaic

Although most of the Old Testament was written in Hebrew, five passages were written in Aramaic, which is very close to Hebrew and also has a twenty-two letter alphabet. The passages are Genesis 31:47, Jeremiah 10:11, Daniel 2:4–7:28, Ezra 4:8–6:18, and Ezra 7:12–26. Aramaic was widely used in the ancient Near East as the language of government, commerce, and trade, especially by the Assyrians, Babylonians, and Persians. It was the *lingua franca,* the common language, of the region until superseded by Greek during the era of the conquests of Alexander the Great. Jesus and the disciples spoke Aramaic, and there are occasional instances of Aramaic words or phrases in the New Testament, such as Jesus' cry from the cross in which he quoted Psalm 22:1: "About the ninth hour Jesus cried out with a loud voice, saying, 'ELI, ELI, LAMA SABACHTHANI?' that is, 'MY GOD, MY GOD, WHY HAVE YOU FORSAKEN ME?'" (Matt. 27:46; Mark 15:34).

Greek

Although Jesus, the disciples, and most early Christians spoke Aramaic (and possibly also Hebrew), the books of the New Testament were written in Greek.

Before his early death, Alexander III of Macedon (356–323 B.C.), commonly known as Alexander the Great, created one of the largest empires of the ancient world through his military conquests. Alexander's empire stretched from Greece through Persia and into India. Through the use of Greek, he unified his government, and Greek became the international language of trade and the vernacular of the Mediterranean region.

Eventually, the regional dialects of Greek gave way to Hellenistic, or *koine* ("common"), Greek. This style of Greek reflected simple, popular language and became the universal dialect of the ancient world from ca. 300 B.C. to A.D. 300. It is the language in which the New Testament was written.

Even after Alexander's empire fell and the Roman Empire emerged, Greek remained the daily language for many people. Although Latin was the official language of the Roman Empire, it was used mainly by the government and military, and in administrative documents. Thus, the writers of the New Testament, such as Paul, were able to write their documents in Greek, knowing that they could be circulated throughout the empire with relative ease and without language barriers. Greek was a cosmopolitan language, easily adaptable to the then-worldwide culture. In much the same sense that English is an international language of commerce and communication today, so was Greek in the first-century world of Jesus. The vocabulary, grammar, and style of *koine* Greek were also integral to the history of the Bible and Bible translation, especially the Greek translation of the Old Testament known as the Septuagint (LXX), dating from about 250–100 B.C.

5. What Bible did Jesus and the apostles use?

The books of the New Testament were yet to be written during the life and ministry of Jesus on earth. It was the Hebrew Scriptures—known to Jews as the Tanak and to Christians today as the Old Testament—that were the Bible of Jesus' day. These were the Scriptures that were in use in the temple and synagogues.

Unlike today when many people own Bibles, personal copies of the Scriptures, in the form of scrolls, were rarely owned by individuals, except for perhaps the extremely wealthy. There were no personal Bibles, only the ones studied and used in the synagogues. Meticulous and accurate memorization of Scripture was common, and it was essential among the illiterate. Thus, the Bible of daily use would have been either the memorized Scriptures or the physical scroll used in the synagogue.[5] The scrolls and Scriptures were highly regarded.

Although Greek was spoken throughout the Roman Empire

in the first century, nevertheless in Jerusalem and the surrounding area where Jesus lived and ministered, Aramaic was the daily language, and Hebrew was the language of the Scriptures read in the temple and synagogues. When Jesus read from the Scriptures in the synagogue in Nazareth, for example (cf. Luke 4:16–20), He read from a Hebrew text and then likely paraphrased in Aramaic. (Such paraphrases and translations, both verbal and written and often accompanied with commentary, were known as *targums*. An example is the category of manuscripts known as the Aramaic Targums.)[6]

A different issue involves quotes from the Old Testament by Jesus and others as recorded in the New Testament. Many of these quotes—especially those found in the gospels of Mark and Luke, which were written for broader audiences than Matthew's primarily Jewish readers—reflect knowledge and usage of the Septuagint. The Septuagint, also known as the LXX, was the Greek translation of the Hebrew Scriptures, and it was used widely outside of Palestine. Of its use, biblical scholars Gleason L. Archer and G. C. Chirichigno write:

> The very reason for using the LXX was rooted in the missionary outreach of the evangelists and apostles of the early church. The LXX translation of the Old Testament had already found its way into every city of the Roman Empire to which the Jews of the Diaspora had gone. It was virtually the only form of the Old Testament in the hands of Jewish believers outside Palestine, and it was certainly the only available form for Gentile converts to the Jewish or Christian faiths.[7]

On the other hand, the special Hebrew Christian readers whom the evangelist Matthew addressed—and even more notably, the recipients of the epistle to the Hebrews—did not require the constant adherence to the LXX that was necessary for Gentile readers.

Hence, Matthew and Hebrews often quote from the Old Testament in a non-LXX form, normally one that is closer to the wording of the Hebrew original.

Jesus, the disciples, and the apostles certainly knew of the Septuagint, but the Scriptures in Hebrew would have been the ones they used. Interestingly, the Dead Sea Scrolls and writings from the Qumran community dating from about 130 B.C. to A.D. 68–73 are in Hebrew, showing the prominent usage of Hebrew during the time of Jesus.

6. Why are there four gospels?

The reader of the New Testament soon notices that the four gospels regarding the life and work of Jesus contain many similarities. However, each gospel also possesses special material not present in the others. This is particularly true of John's gospel, which is 98 percent unique.

The question that naturally arises is, why are there four gospels instead of one (or three, or five)? The question is impossible to answer since there is no practical or theological requirement for a certain number. All of the words and events recorded among the four gospels could certainly have been contained in just one writing. This is evident from both Church history and recent time. During the second century, in the Syrian branch of the church, a theologian by the name of Tatian blended all four gospels into one account called the Diatessaron (Greek for "through four"). He made all accounts to harmonize, removing any differences among the accounts. This *harmony* ("seeing as one") is different from a *synopsis* (from the Greek, "seeing together"), which describes the canonical gospels. In the Syrian church, Tatian's Diatessaron lasted until the fifth century, until it was finally replaced by the four Gospels in the Syrian Peshitta.

Johnston M. Cheney, in *The Life of Christ in Stereo,* made a more recent attempt at creating a single, unified account.[8] While such attempts furnish an easy and continuous flow of the life of

Christ and to some degree remove difficulties in the text, the four Gospels have provided a critical service in the development of Christianity from the mid-first century A.D. until the present. The four approaches to Christ's words and works provided accounts that resonated with readers of the Jewish, Roman, and Greek worlds, presenting aspects of Jesus that made sense to them in their distinct cultural settings. These were not contradictory presentations, but views of Jesus that portrayed the many sides of Jesus' full-orbed person.

We see this first in Matthew's gospel. It was most likely addressed to Jews in Antioch of Syria, who understood the link between Jesus the Messiah and Jesus the hope of Israel as Son of Abraham and Son of David. These Jews no doubt had questions regarding the anticipated future of Israel that would occur when Messiah came. Since this future had not yet arrived, Matthew broadened his readers' understanding to realize that Messiah's coming, death, and resurrection also embraced the Gentiles, culminating with the Great Commission to disciple the non-Jewish world.

Mark's gospel was for the Roman, who would hardly have understood or appreciated the beginning of Matthew with its genealogy. Instead, Mark presented Jesus as the servant of God who came to serve humanity and redeem all people. The fast pace of the book would have appealed to the Roman mentality.

The gospel of Luke revealed a real man, a perfect man, and a Savior. The physician Luke was interested in Jesus as a person of compassion who cared for the poor, the sick, the disenfranchised, and women. Jesus was a man worth following and emulating.

John's gospel, as indicated earlier, was almost entirely different from the others. Why is this so? John wrote his gospel possibly thirty to forty years after the other gospels. Those gospels, or the oral traditions on which they were built, had traveled throughout much of the Roman world. So in writing his own gospel, why would John have simply repeated what others had already said? In chapter twenty, John indicated that Jesus did many other things—presumably such as found in the other gospels—that John did not include in his writing. Rather, John provided much new material, especially discourses of Jesus, which the other gospel writers did not mention.

Moreover, John painted a picture of Jesus as the Son of God, the Savior of all humanity. The person Jesus was both God and man. He was eternal with the Father, yet He tabernacled among humans to show them the way to God the Father through Himself.

Through the Gospels, God chose to reveal His Son in four ways: as Messiah King, as Suffering Servant, as Perfect Man, and as God in the flesh. Only with this full-orbed view of Jesus do we really come to understand who He is, and the four Gospels give us such a view.

PART 2

The Organization of the Bible

7. Why are there two Testaments and what are they?

The Bible is composed of two sections which we have designated the Old Testament and the New Testament. Due to this nomenclature, many Christians have ignored the Old Testament, believing that the New Testament has replaced this portion of Scripture.

In reality, the New Testament does not replace the Old Testament but builds upon it. Jesus and the apostles considered the Law, Prophets, and Writings to be the Word of God (2 Tim. 3:16–17), having come from the very mouth of God. It was useful for teaching doctrine, reproving, correcting, and instructing in righteousness. Yet rarely in the Christian church today is the Old Testament proclaimed from the pulpit or read by the average Christian, other than perhaps the Psalms and Proverbs. Most attention is given to portions of the New Testament, such as the letters of Paul.

Why is the Old Testament so ignored? One reason may be that we believe Jesus fulfilled the Law and Prophets and so has made the "Old" Testament antiquated and unneeded. Since Christ's death has brought salvation to us, the regulations given to the Jewish people and the ceremonial practices of the Jewish religion seem irrelevant to us. But this is a half-truth. It is true that many of the laws given to Israel are not needed and that the temple worship is now set aside, since these things served only to lead us to Christ. But much of the moral code of Israel is still in force in the New Testament, and Jesus and the apostles relied heavily on the biblical text we call the Old Testament to determine the manner of life that Christians should live and the doctrine they should believe. For example, Jesus' teaching on loving one's neighbor as oneself is considered a new teaching of Christ in contrast to the Law, but in reality, He quotes the book of Leviticus for this truth.

The Hebrew Scriptures lead us to the Messiah, but most of their truths teach us about God and a biblical worldview, sometimes even more fully than parts of the New Testament. The apostles presupposed knowledge of the Old Testament; they did not feel the need to restate everything and certainly not to replace everything. They built on the truth given in the Old Testament to provide teaching to the church.

The New Testament teaching of God remains consistent with what is found in the Hebrew Scriptures, and the Old Testament's moral teaching given to humans remains true. Moreover, the Old Testament (some prefer "Former Testament") contains hundreds of prophecies yet to be fulfilled, many of which are taught in the New Testament, but not to the same depth as in the Old Testament.

Consider the things in the New Testament that make no sense unless we refer to the Old Testament. The gospels speak of Abraham, as do the letters of Paul, but what can we really know about the man and the covenant he made with God apart from reading the Old Testament? Peter, and briefly Jesus, speaks of the flood of Noah; but without the Old Testament, we can understand little about the event and its cause, purpose, and aftermath. One could continue with a hundred other illustrations, but the point is clear: we need the entire Bible in order to understand the revelation of God to humanity.

There are two testimonies of God's working among His people.

The Old Testament sets forth His plans to redeem fallen humanity and to establish a kingdom on the earth through a redeemer-king. The New Testament reveals this redeemer-king as Jesus the Messiah. The salvation offered through Jesus is presented in detail in the New Testament. The earthly kingdom of God anticipated in the covenants and prophecies of the Old Testament is taught by Jesus and the apostles, but it is yet to be completely fulfilled.

Without recognizing, appreciating, and using both Testaments, we lack the full counsel of God regarding Himself, human duty and blessings, and God's plan for the future.

8. How are the Hebrew Scriptures organized and why?

The order and division of the Hebrew Scriptures differs from the Christian Old Testament, although the material is the same. All of the books of the Bible, both Old and New Testaments, were written and circulated separately; yet their divine inspiration and unique character were progressively recognized such that they received special care.

The Hebrew Scriptures are listed in three groupings: Law (Torah), Prophets (Nebi'im), and Writings (Kethubim). These groupings are mentioned in the Apocryphal writing of Ecclesiasticus (also known as the Wisdom of ben Sirach 49:8–10, 44–50), which dates from 200–180 B.C. The Prologue to Ecclesiasticus (sometimes known as the Wisdom of Jesus, Son of Sirach), which was written about 132 B.C., also notes this threefold division.[1] The most commonly cited record of the division is the first-century A.D. (C.E.) citation from the work *Contra Apion* (1.37–43) by Josephus.[2] Josephus writes of twenty-two books. They are the same as the twenty-four currently used, combining Judges-Ruth and Jeremiah-Lamentations. (These twenty-two books also correspond to the thirty-nine of the Protestant Christian Old Testament.) The number of books as twenty-four is found in the Apocryphal book 2 Esdras 14:44–48 (also called 4 Ezra).

The books of the three groupings are listed in the following chart.

The New Testament speaks of a threefold structure of the Jewish Scriptures in the words of Jesus: "These are My words which I spoke to you while I was still with you, that all things which are written about Me in the Law of Moses and the Prophets and the Psalms must be fulfilled" (Luke 24:44). The designation *Psalms* probably refers to all of the Writings (Kethubim), of which Psalms is the largest book. There are also several other New Testament verses that speak of a twofold rather than threefold structure (e.g., Matt. 5:17; Luke 16:16–17).

Order of the Old Testament			
Hebrew Bible	Torah Law	Nebi'im Prophets	Kethubim Writings
(The Tanak) (24 books)	Genesis	Joshua	Psalms
	Exodus	Judges	Proverbs
	Leviticus	Samuel (1 and 2)	Job
	Numbers	Kings (1 and 2)	Song of Songs
	Deuteronomy	Isaiah	Ruth
		Jeremiah	Lamentations
	(5 books)	Minor Prophets	Ecclesiastes
		Ezekiel	Esther
		Hosea	Daniel
		Joel	Ezra
		Amos	Nehemiah
		Obadiah	Chronicles (1 and 2)
		Jonah	
		Micah	(12 book)
		Nahum	
		Habakkuk	
		Zephaniah	
		Haggai	
		Zechariah	
		Malachi	
		(7 books)	

Septuagint (27 books)	Torah	History	Poetry	Prophets
	Genesis	Joshua	Psalms (and	The Twelve
	Exodus	Judges	Odes**)	(Minor
	Leviticus	Ruth	Proverbs	Prophets)
	Numbers	1 Kings	Ecclesiastes	Hosea
	Deuteronomy	(1 Samuel)	Canticles	Amos
		2 Kings	(Song of Songs)	Micah
	(5 books)	(2 Samuel)	Job	Joel
		3 Kings	Wisdom of	Obadiah
		(1 Kings)	Solomon*	Jonah
		4 Kings	Sirach*	Nahum
		(2 Kings)	Psalms of	Habakkuk
		1 Chronicles	Solomon*	Zephaniah
		2 Chronicles		Malachi
		1 Esdras*	(8 books)	Isaiah
		2 Esdras*		Jeremiah
		(Ezra–		Lamentations
		Nehemiah)		Epistle of
		Esther		Jeremiah*
		Judith*		Ezekiel
		Tobit*		Susanna*
		1 Maccabees*		Daniel*
		2 Maccabees*		Bel and the
		3 Maccabees*		Dragon
		4 Maccabees*		
				(9 books)

*Apocryphal books
**Prayers used in the Orthodox Church from Old and New Testament and so unusual to have in the LXX

The divisions are made on the basis of grouping the five books of Moses (the Pentateuch), the writings of the Major Prophets and Minor Prophets (including Joshua, Judges, Samuel, and Kings as early prophets), and other wisdom and historical works (including Daniel as primarily history rather than prophecy). Modern Hebrew

Bibles contain thirty-six books, breaking Ezra-Nehemiah into two and listing each of the twelve Minor Prophets rather than using the previous designation, Book of the Twelve. In the Christian categorization of the Jewish Scriptures, there are the categories of Law, Historical Books, Poetry, and Prophets, totaling thirty-nine books.

Sometimes the Jewish Scriptures are referred to as the Tanak. This designation is an acrostic using the first letter from each of three groupings—T from Torah, N from Nebi'im, and K from Kethubim, and then inserting the vowel A twice.

9. How are the Greek Scriptures organized and why?

The history of the organization of the New Testament Greek Scriptures—separate from the Old Testament Greek Scriptures known as the Septuagint—is much easier to trace than the organization of the Hebrew Scriptures (Old Testament). The New Testament begins with the four gospels, which center on the life and ministry of Jesus Christ. These four books provide the foundation for all that follows. They follow the traditional Greek order of the Gospels, with Matthew, the first of the four, being the gospel that is understood to best make the transition for the reader from the Old Testament to the New Testament. (A couple of variations exist within some churches such as the Coptic Church, which has an order of John, Matthew, Mark, and Luke.)[3]

Following the four gospels is the Book of Acts, which provides a history of the early church and serves as a transition from the life and ministry of Jesus Christ to the rest of the New Testament. Though most manuscripts place Acts after the Gospels, there is some variation, such as the fourth century manuscript Codex Sinaiticus that places Acts between Philemon and James.

After the Book of Acts come the Epistles—letters written to the early church by the apostle Paul during his missionary journeys. These are listed primarily according to their length, with Romans coming first as the longest of the letters and 2 Thessalonians coming last as the shortest of them (though there has been some variation through the centuries regarding their order). The Epistles are followed by Hebrews, after which come letters addressed to individuals according to length (1 and 2 Timothy, Titus, and Philemon). These four letters are followed by the three letters of John, followed by Jude, and finally, by Revelation. Last of the New Testament books to be written, Revelation presents the prophetic culmination of human history.[4]

10. How is the English Bible organized and why?

The organization of the books of the Bible in English translations differs between Protestant, Roman Catholic, and Eastern Orthodox editions. While all of them divide the text into Old and New Testaments, they vary on the number of books accepted into their lists for the Old Testament. Protestants hold to thirty-nine books, Roman Catholics hold to forty-six books and Eastern Orthodox Christians hold to fifty-one books. The differences are due to acceptance or rejection of the books of the Apocrypha and how many books are understood to be part of that collection. The Jewish Scriptures (Tanak) contain the same thirty-nine books as the Protestant Old Testament, although there is variation in the order of the writings, and the books of the twelve Minor Prophets are compiled into one book in the Jewish text known simply as The Twelve. The following chart shows the three major lists of Old Testament books.

In the organization of the New Testament, all Christians list the four gospels first since the person and work of Jesus Christ, including His birth, death, resurrection, and ascension, are the foundation of Christianity. However, there is some variation in the order of the Gospels; for instance, Coptic churches (Egypt) list the order as John, Matthew, Mark, and Luke, and some Western churches follow the order Matthew, John, Luke, and Mark, as does the fifth-century document Codex Bezae.

The more common order of Matthew, Mark, Luke, and John is

based on the idea that Matthew provides the best transition from the Old Testament to the New Testament. This is then followed by the Book of Acts giving the early history of the church (although even here there is variation with Codex Sinaiticus, a fourth-century Greek manuscript containing part the Old Testament of all of the New Testament, listing Acts after Philemon).

Following the book of Acts in the English text are the letters of Paul written to various churches and normally listed in order of length (though again with variation in some early manuscripts). These are then followed by letters to individuals (with the exception of Hebrews) and conclude with Jude and then Revelation.

Divisions of the English Bible[5]				
Old Testament (39 books)	**Law**	**History**	**Wisdom and Poetry**	**Prophets**
	Genesis–Deuteronomy (5 books)	Joshua–Esther (12 books)	Job–Song of Songs (5 books)	Isaiah–Malachi (17 books)
New Testament (27 books)	**Gospel**	**History**	**Letters**	**Apocalypse**
	Matthew–John (4 books)	Acts (1 book)	Romans–Jude (21 books)	Revelation (1 book)

11. Who divided the Bible into verses and chapters and when?

Verse and chapter divisions were not part of the original manuscripts of the Bible but were added later for ease in reading and study. This became especially important as the books were collected into a canon and unified volume, making it necessary to distinguish one book from another.

Verse divisions of the Old Testament were added very early, but variations existed based upon different scribal centers. Standardization of the Old Testament verses was set by the scribes of the ben Asher family of the Masoretes about A.D. 900. Chapter divisions in the Bible are very late to the history of the Bible as a book. Present-day chapter divisions were first added by Stephen Langton (1150–1228). Langton, the Archbishop of Canterbury, England, added the divisions in a copy of the Latin Vulgate. These divisions, with some adjustments, were later transferred to the Old Testament Hebrew text by Salomon ben Ishmael (ca. 1330). We know there were adjustments because chapter divisions in the English Bible and the Hebrew Bible differ in some places, with the English divisions sometimes separating literary units and hindering the meaning. (See, for example, Gen. 1:1–2:4 and Pss. 42–43.)

For the New Testament, versification was not as uniform, and different divisions for both chapters and verses arose over the centuries for different books of the New Testament. Among the first means of distinguishing verses were not numbered passages, but marks inserted by various scribes in their own books and copying efforts. However, the marks were not uniform within duplicate copies of the same book, and there was no universal marking system. For example, in the latter half of the sixth century A.D., Archbishop Andrew of Caesarea in Cappadocia (central Turkey) divided the book of Revelation into twenty-four parts because of the twenty-four elders mentioned in Revelation 4:4. He then further divided the twenty-four parts into seventy-two parts because each elder had a body, soul, and spirit. Earlier scribes in the fourth century inserted section marks into the four gospels, as seen in the Codex Vaticanus. However, as with the Old Testament, it was the work of Stephen Langton that gave chapter divisions to the Latin Vulgate, which were subsequently added to English translations.[6]

The first person to divide New Testament chapters into verses was the Italian Dominican biblical scholar Santi Pagnini (1470–1541). However, his versification system was never widely adopted. The verse divisions used today in the New Testament are the result of the work of Robert Estienne (1503–1559). Known as Robertus

Stephanus in Latin and Robert Stephen in English, Estienne was a sixteenth-century printer and classical scholar in Paris. Late in his life, he converted from Roman Catholicism to Protestantism and was the first to print the Bible divided into a standard number format. Estienne created a numbering in his 1551 edition of the Greek and Latin New Testament, which he published in Geneva. He also used this same numbering in his 1553 publication of the Bible in French.[7]

The first English New Testament to use Estienne's verse divisions was a 1557 translation by William Whittingham (ca. 1524–1579). The first Bible in English to use both chapters and verses was the very popular Geneva Bible published shortly afterward in 1560. These verse divisions soon gained acceptance as a standard way to notate verse and have since been used in nearly all English Bibles.

PART 3

The Uniqueness of the Bible

12. Why is there a Bible?

The book that we call the Bible has not always existed. It has come down to us today through a very long process that began in the fifteenth century B.C., originating as the first five books of the Hebrew Scriptures written in an early form of Hebrew script. Gradually, additional books were added to the Hebrew Bible by prophets and kings called by God to write down the revelations He gave them and the thoughts and events they experienced in their interactions with Him.

Prior to the written text, God had revealed Himself only to a few, beginning with Adam and Eve, then others such as Enoch, Noah, Abraham, Isaac, and Jacob. Upon His deliverance of the children of Israel from Egyptian captivity through Moses, Yahweh established a special covenantal relationship with His people and gave to them their history and law in the five books of Moses, the Pentateuch. As He continued to live among His people, God revealed Himself more and more, speaking to them through the prophets, who wrote down many of their revelations for a perpetual record. By the time of Ezra and Nehemiah after the Babylonian captivity, Yahweh had given twenty-two books (thirty-nine in the

English Bible) that recounted His interactions with humankind and the people of Israel in particular. Nothing more needed to be said until the coming of the promised Messiah, so He remained silent for four hundred years.

With the fullness of times and the birth of His Son, God once more moved His kingdom and redemptive intent forward. The words of Jesus and their implications became the basis of the New Testament. Rather than relying only on a national people to obey His law, God set forth His intention to save all of humanity, with Jesus commanding His disciples to move beyond Israel to offer God's redemption to all nations. The words and acts of Jesus and the apostles became the basis for recording additional books, specifically the Gospels, the Acts of the apostles, and the letters and treatises of the apostles.

We have the Bible because of God's desire to provide a more permanent record of His acts and words among human beings, one that could be shared and remembered by large numbers of people. Both in its entirety and in parts, the Bible has been translated into hundreds of languages and impacted millions of people, far beyond what a personal revelation to a few people could ever accomplish.

13. How did God communicate His revelation to humanity?

How does an infinite God who is invisible and immaterial communicate with finite humans in a physical world? Certainly one way is through the natural world, as spoken of by the psalmist in Psalms 19 and 119 and by the apostle Paul in Romans 1:18–23. This manner of divine communication, called *natural revelation*, consists of the celestial universe and God's operations on the earth through such means as rain and storms.

In the biblical text, however, God uses written words to communicate—words that have come to us through, or as a record of, miraculous events, visible manifestations, and divine speech.

Miraculous Events

God reveals Himself to human beings by causing historical events to unfold in certain ways that affect human history. In Genesis 12, Yahweh called Abraham to travel to an unfamiliar land in order to give it to him and his physical descendants through Isaac. God did so to reveal His being and His purposes for humanity, and He did it at the crossroads of three continents—Europe, Asia, and Africa. The world's nations had to travel through this small piece of land as they dealt with each other in trade and in war. This allowed the Hebrews to teach, through word and example, that God the Creator invited all peoples to know Him. Moreover, when the Israelites disobeyed God, their disobedience provided an opportunity for God to teach lessons about His holiness, justice, and wrath toward those who are disobedient.

With the birth of Isaac (Gen. 21) and later Jacob (Gen. 25), Yahweh disclosed His continuing intention to fulfill His promises to Abraham through his physical descendants (Gen. 15, 17). This single-mindedness on the part of God shows that He is a faithful deity, loyal to His chosen people and faithful to His spoken word.

One revelation of God that continues to be remembered among the Jewish people is the Passover event and the inauguration of its observance (Exod. 11–12). Pharaoh, through his decree in Exodus 1:16, intended the death of newborn males of Israel for ill, but God used the occasion of the Passover to bring judgment on Egypt and bless Israel. Yahweh revealed to the Hebrews and to Egypt that He would deliver His people because of His promises to Abraham, Isaac, and Jacob. The Passover feast remembers that the death angel that passed through Egypt distinguished between the firstborn sons of Israel and those of the Egyptians. The firstborn of Israel, then, became holy to Yahweh and symbolic of the "firstfruits" of God's people who are dedicated to Him.

Another example of God's disclosing His deliverance and love of Israel is the miraculous opening and crossing of the Red Sea. Exodus 13:17–14:29 tells the story of how God protected the Hebrews from the Egyptian army by means of a pillar of fire and then opened the sea for them to escape from the Egyptians. The sea stood on either side like a wall as the Israelites walked across on dry ground. The songsters of Israel sang that Yahweh piled up the waters with the blast of His nostrils; then after the children of Israel had passed to the other shore, He covered the Egyptian army and Pharaoh with the returning waters (Exod. 15:1–18).

Divine Speech

Besides using events to communicate, God also does so through human language. Obviously, the all-knowing triune God does not need to use language within the Godhead, but in order to reveal Himself to humans, He meets us at our level by speaking in human language that we can comprehend. Sometimes His speech is audible; at other times, He speaks through the mouths of the prophets, or in dreams and visions; and finally, and most clearly, He speaks through Scripture.

Though God may have communicated mind-to-mind with persons like Adam, Abraham, and Samuel, there is good reason to believe that He spoke to them audibly. When Adam and Abraham responded to the "voice" of God, the natural reading of the text is that they did so audibly. In other places in the Bible where God spoke to humans, the text indicates that an actual voice was heard. Compare, for example, the occasion when God spoke audibly to Samuel when he was in the tabernacle (1 Sam. 3). The New Testament also records two occasions when God spoke audibly from heaven at the baptism of Jesus (Matt. 3:16–17; Luke 3:21–22) and on the Mount of Transfiguration (Matt. 17:1–9; Mark 9:7; Luke 9:28–36).

God also speaks through the mouths of prophets. In fact, the primary word used in the Old Testament for *prophet* (*nābî'*) means "mouth" and was used because these persons were the very mouthpieces of God. "Thus says Yahweh" is a common phrase found throughout the Old Testament books of prophecy.

Another way that God spoke audibly to humans was in dreams. The most famous dreamers and interpreters of divine communications were Daniel and Joseph. God gave specific words to them, and He also gave them the interpretation of dreams.

Similar to dreams were visions. The two most striking differences between them are that a vision, unlike a dream, was seen when one was awake, and a vision seems to have been more stark and spectacular, though this is uncertain.

Last of all, divine speech is present in the original manuscripts of the New Testament, and to the degree that the transcription, transmission, and translation of these words is accurate, we have the content of those manuscripts available to us. Unlike the former examples of divine speech, God's words in Scripture are not audible from God. Yet they carry the greatest clarity and force.

Visible Manifestations

The third manner in which God communicates with humans is by visibly manifesting Himself. For example, Yahweh appeared as a burning bush to Moses, and even as the *shekinah* glory (Exod. 3:2–4; 24:15–18; 40:34–35).

The most helpful way in which God revealed Himself, however, is when He took human form. One of these occurrences is when the Angel of Yahweh appeared to Sarah's maid, Hagar, after she had fled from Sarah's home. The Angel told her to return to Sarah and promised her that her son, Ishmael, would become great (Gen. 16:7–14). Another such appearance was to Jacob. A man encountered him during the night, and Jacob wrestled with the man throughout the night. The man then promised to bless him and told Jacob that he had striven with God. Jacob realized that he had fought with God, and therefore he named the place Peniel, which means "face of God" (Gen. 32:24–30).

Another major occurrence of God taking human form is in Genesis 18, when three men came to the tent of Abraham in the heat of the day. Abraham had his wife prepare a meal for them, which they ate with him after their feet were washed. After the meal, two of the men went down to Sodom to destroy it while the third man stayed to have a conversation with Abraham. The final verse of the chapter says, "As soon as He had finished speaking to Abraham the LORD departed, and Abraham returned to his place" (Gen. 18:33). The man who had his feet washed, who ate Abraham's food, and who talked with Abraham at length, was none other than Yahweh Himself.

The ultimate example of visible manifestations is when the eternal God came to us in the flesh in the person of Jesus (John 1:14; 1 John 1:1–3). The second person of the triune God revealed the character of the Father as only the eternal Son could do (John 1:18; 14:9). The Son was the best communication that God could offer to man. As the author of Hebrews so eloquently states, "God, after He spoke long ago to the fathers in the prophets in many portions and in many ways, in these last days has spoken to us in His Son, whom He appointed heir of all things, through whom also He made the world. And He is the radiance of His glory and the exact representation of His nature, and upholds all things by the word of His power" (Heb. 1:1–3).

14. What is meant by the terms *inspiration*, *infallibility*, and *inerrancy* when referring to the Bible?

There are three words regularly used in speaking of the quality or character of the Bible, namely, *inspiration*, *infallibility*, and *inerrancy*. Each of these is a unique term that supports the trustworthiness of Holy Scripture, and each should be understood to refer to the Bible as originally given by God.

Inspiration

The term *inspiration* is firmly established in the minds of the general public and the community of scholars, so it is unlikely to change. It comes from the Latin term *inspirare*, meaning, "to breathe into." According to Paul's teaching in 2 Timothy, however, the Scripture is *theopneustos*—that is, breathed *out* by God. Some teach that when a person reads the Scripture, God inspires the reader; in actuality, though, when one reads the Bible, he or she is reading what God *ex*pired, or breathed out of His mouth. The apostle Peter explained that scriptural prophecies originated with the Holy Spirit, not with the prophets who recorded them. Peter wrote, "Above all, you do well if you recognize this: No prophecy of scripture ever comes about by the prophet's own imagination, for no prophecy was ever borne of human impulse; rather, men carried along by the Holy Spirit spoke from God" (2 Peter 1:20–21 NET).

The Bible teaches that each and every word of the original writings of the Hebrew and Greek Scriptures came from God, and that the whole of Scripture came from God.

Infallibility

Since the Bible comes from the very mouth of God, then it cannot deceive, which is the essential meaning of the word *infallible*. The word comes from the two Latin words *in*, which means "not," and *fallere*, which means "deceive." God is faithful and truthful, and He will not attempt to communicate anything contrary to His own nature. The Bible says it is impossible for God to lie.

Sometimes people confuse the word *infallible* with the word *inerrant*, but the two words describe different aspects of God's trustworthy character. Infallibility does not simply mean that the Bible has no error; rather, the word signifies that the Bible has no possibility of error, because God is its ultimate author.

Inerrancy

Whereas inspiration speaks of the activity of God in producing Scripture, and infallibility indicates the inability of Scripture to lie because God is its author, *inerrancy* addresses the result of inspiration and infallibility: the Scripture has no error. When we speak of inerrancy, we are referring to the actual autograph written by the prophets and apostles, not to any subsequent copy of the Hebrew and Greek text, into which human error may be introduced. The original manuscripts were superintended by the Holy Spirit in producing a document free from factual errors.

Inerrancy makes room for literary devices such as exaggeration, or euphemisms that avoid sensitive language, or approximations in the use of numbers or locations. All of these are common to the normal use of language and were easily recognizable by the ancient readers of the Scripture as well as the authors. Once all the facts are known, it becomes clear that the Scriptures do not err.

One might object that since humans are sinful and fallible, everything that touches humanity must be as well. We offer two responses. First, in Numbers 22, when the pagan prophet Balaam attempted to curse Israel in return for payment from Balak, the king of Moab, he could not; he could only say the words that God put into his mouth. If a pagan prophet *had* to speak the word of God, then surely the holy prophets and apostles of God would do so.

Secondly, when the eternal Son of God took upon Himself the finite form of a man, He was kept without sin by the Spirit of God. Surely fallible humans carried along by the same Spirit could produce the infallible and inerrant words of God.

15. How reliable is the biblical teaching regarding history, theology, science, and ethics?

Often, the Bible is brought into question by those who claim that the biblical texts and teachings are not accurate with regard to matters of history, theology, science, and ethics. These claims are made because the critic finds a text, or texts, of Scripture that are incongruent from what contemporary naysayers believe is the truth. To disprove the Bible's trustworthiness, the biblical text is sometimes subjected to a Herculean standard that denies its human communicative form.

For example, can every historical person or event mentioned in the Bible be substantiated by some ancient literary reference or supported by an archaeological find? The answer is no. Do many theological statements made by one author of Scripture appear to be in contradiction to a statement by another author? The answer is yes. What about science? Is the terminology of the ancient world different from that of the modern scientific world? Surely, and we would set the Bible aside in a moment were it written using contemporary terms, for it would not then be an ancient book. Finally, do the ethics and morals of the twenty-first century appear to be very different from what we observe in the biblical text, and sometimes more sensitive to social justice? Yes, at times. This is certainly true as we observe the presence of slavery in the biblical world, or the status of women, or the execution of individuals because of certain crimes, or the destruction of the Canaanites in war.

All of these concerns rightly need to be addressed, but the Bible is not under a legitimate indictment once we put them in perspective. The first thing we must understand before approaching these issues is that the Bible is not one thing, but many. It is a book of history, but it is also a book of theology, with neither area of knowledge detracting from the other. Moreover, the Bible incorporates various literary styles, including narrative and poetry, proverbs and riddles, letters and prophecy. Each kind of literature must be read and understood for what it is, not as if it were something else. Also, different styles are often integrated in the biblical passages. For example, a passage with metaphorical language may be surrounded by non-metaphorical language. The reader must adapt accordingly, just as with contemporary literature, in order to accurately understand the text.

What about seeming contradictions in matters of history, theology, science, and ethics with specific biblical texts? Denying that some biblical texts appear to conflict with these areas of knowledge is unfruitful. However, the more we know about historical data and scientific proofs, the more the Bible is vindicated.

The Bible and History

The Bible has withstood numerous charges of historical inaccuracy. For instance, until the late nineteenth century, critics of the Bible argued that a people known as the Hittites never existed. Then the Hittite nation, one of the greatest empires of the ancient world, was discovered in southeastern Turkey. Similarly, liberal scholars denied that David, the king of Israel, was anything more than a legendary hero; but then at Tel Dan, in northern Israel, an Aramaic inscription was found that contained a reference to the house of David.

Critics once claimed that Caiaphas the high priest was just a literary device used by the gospel writers to represent a foe of Jesus. Now, however, we know of Caiaphas's house and have his ossuary (bone box). Luke has been questioned regarding numerous matters; yet in examining his understanding of towns, rulers, terms, and the like, various scholars have shown his record to be amazingly accurate. The list could continue for hundreds of examples.

The Bible and Theology

Do some biblical passages contradict each other? Often this claim is made regarding how one biblical author records a passage one way while another records it differently. Not only are biblical texts supposedly pitted against each other, but so are biblical writers. For example, Paul and James are said to hold different views of justification, Paul by faith and James by works.

The Synoptic Gospels in particular—Matthew, Mark, and Luke—are said to contain contradictions. But the Gospels simply present the life of Christ from four different vantage points and for different purposes. Each account is similar to the others in some ways and different in others; each both includes and excludes material that appears in the others. This is to be expected from authentic eyewitness records. Were they word-for-word at every point, the authors would clearly have been copying each other's work and perhaps colluding among themselves. Instead, the Gospels bear the mark of authentic accounts of the life of Christ from different people.[1]

As far as theological disagreement, we should understand that the New Testament writers have different emphases in their respective books and present the truths of Christianity in different terms. For example, when Paul uses the expression "salvation by faith," he is saying that faith is the medium through which God dispenses His grace to us apart from any works that we have done. When James, on the other hand, speaks of "justification by works" and of our not being saved apart from works, he focuses on the kinds of deeds that reveal the work of faith in the Christian's spirit. The authors are not in contradiction but are using their terms and expressions differently.

The Bible and Science

Though science as we know it originated within the Christian community, many modern scientists have been formidable opponents of Scripture.[2] They maintain that the Bible was written in a pre-scientific world, and its statements about the physical world are often inaccurate. The Bible is said to view the world as flat and having four corners, with hell beneath us and heaven above us, where in fact we are on a globe with no true down and up. Stephen Hawking, the Isaac Newton Professor of Physics at the University of Cambridge, has boldly said that there is no hell. Scoffers laugh at the biblical references to the rising and setting of the sun, as if the sun revolved around the earth. In particular, belief in a special creation of humanity in the persons of Adam and Eve is viewed as archaic.

How does a Christian respond to such charges?[3] First, we need to acknowledge that the Bible does refer to the rising of the sun and the four corners of the earth. But how were those terms understood in the biblical world, and are they understood any differently in common speech today? None of us believe that the sun circles around the earth, yet we use such figures of speech. They are phenomenological in nature—that is, they describe how things appear to us. From our frame of reference, the sun seems to rise and set.

"Four corners of the earth" is a directional term similar to north, south, east, and west. It doesn't imply that there are four actual corners. Though certainly some have believed in a flat earth, this was not generally true in the Middle Ages or in educated Greek society from the sixth century B.C. on, starting with Pythagoras. This holds true for the biblical text as well. When Isaiah writes, "It is He who sits above the circle of the earth, and its inhabitants are like grasshoppers, Who stretches out the heavens like a curtain and spreads them out like a tent to dwell in" (Isa. 40:22), the prophet is clearly speaking poetically and metaphorically, not literally.

The major clash between non-theistic science and the Christian view of the world relates to the theory of Darwinian evolution. Yet many scientists have not embraced the macro-evolutionary aspect of the theory that human beings have evolved from a common ancestor to human beings—or, on a related note, that the universe occurred by accident.[4]

The Bible and Ethics

One of the most troublesome elements in Scripture is the moral failures of the people of God. The incestuous affair between Judah and Tamar is disturbing, as is the adultery of David with Bathsheba and his subsequent murder of Bathsheba's husband, Uriah. And what of God's own actions? What of His destruction of the world in the time of Noah, or his command to the Israelites to exterminate the Canaanites? What are we to think of these accounts of God's judgment?

Unlike other ancient literatures that hide flaws and failures of leaders, the Bible does not hide the sinfulness of God's people. Rather, it reveals God's judgment against sin and those who commit it, and it also demonstrates His forgiveness for His people.

As for the destruction of gross sinners like the Canaanites and the world of Noah's time, it must be remembered that God's creatures are responsible to their Creator. There is no inherent right to life apart from the grace and benefit of God. God is longsuffering, giving humans ample opportunity to repent of their sins. The Canaanites had 400 years to do so (Gen. 15:13, 14, 16). The people of Noah's day heard his preaching for 120 years and yet did not repent (Gen. 6:3, 7).[5]

16. How is the Bible similar to and different from other religious texts?

Almost all religions have writings that are considered sacred and which adherents of a given faith use for personal and corporate guidance and worship. Hinduism has the *Vedas,* the *Upanishads,* and the *Bhagavad Gita.* Islam proclaims the *Qur'an* as its written authority, and Buddhists use the *Tripitaka.* In Sikhism, the most important text is the *Sri Guru Granth Sahib,* and in the ancient Persian faith Zoroastrianism, the central holy book is the *Avesta.*

Some sacred texts are the collected sayings and proverbs of the founder or other spiritual leaders of the faith tradition. Other texts provide lengthy narratives, biographies, or guidance for doctrine and practice.

Christianity is no exception. It too has sacred writings—the books that comprise the Bible. On one level, a sociological level, the Bible is similar to other sacred texts. It provides guidance for Christians with respect to matters of faith and practice. It tells of the early history of Christianity in the book of Acts, and it gives the long history of the Jewish people and the faith out of which Christianity emerged.

What is unique about the sacred Scripture of Christianity, the Bible, are the truth claims contained within its pages. Though written over many centuries with many authors, styles, and genres in three languages on three continents, the Bible claims to be the revealed Word of God, divinely inspired.[6] As such, it is the most important book in the world. There is no getting around the fact of the Bible's claims to truth and exclusivity. That is where it differs from the sacred writings of other religions. And that is where there is an unbridgeable theological chasm between Christianity and other religions. Only in the Bible do we find the offer of eternal life and salvation (John 3:16). While the Bible shares some sociological similarities with other sacred texts, its presuppositions, statements, and teachings give it theological dissimilarity with other sacred texts.

More than 3,800 times in the Bible, we find declarations such as, "God spoke," or, "Then the Yahweh said," or "Hear the word of Yahweh," (e.g., Exod. 14:1; 20:1; Lev. 4:1; Deut. 4:2; 32:48; Isa. 1:10). Among the many verses teaching the divine inspiration and unique character of the Bible are several significant New Testament verses:

Sanctify them in the truth; Your word is truth. (John 17:17)

Now we have received, not the spirit of the world, but the Spirit who is from God, so that we may know the things freely given to us by God, which things we also speak, not in words taught by human wisdom, but in those taught by the Spirit, combining spiritual *thoughts* with spiritual *words*. (1 Cor. 2:12–13, emphasis added)

All Scripture is inspired by God and profitable for teaching, for reproof, for correction, [and] for training in righteousness. (2 Tim. 3:16)

God, after He spoke long ago to the fathers in the prophets in many portions and in many ways, in these last days has spoken to us in His Son, whom He appointed heir of all things, through whom also He made the world. (Heb. 1:1–2)

No prophecy was ever made by an act of human will, but men moved by the Holy Spirit spoke from God. (2 Peter 1:21)

The Bible claims to be the verbal, infallible, and inerrant Word of God given to humanity. It is authoritative, and its authority extends to every verse and portion of itself. Christians believe that God inspired the Bible. By this, we understand inspiration to mean that God superintended and guided the Bible's human authors so that they composed and recorded without error in the original manuscripts God's message to humanity, each author doing so within his own style.[7] Not all Christians agree with our understanding of the nature of the Bible, but we believe that if one reads and studies the text carefully, the inspiration and authority of the Bible is clearly taught within it.

As noted above, the competing truth claims of Christianity as recorded in the Bible are many and exclusive.[8] The Bible offers a sure and certain guide for us that speaks directly or indirectly to every area of life. And it tells us not only of this life, but also of the possibility of eternal life through faith in Jesus Christ. Such a claim is controversial, but it is also true.

The longest of the 150 psalms in the Old Testament book of Psalms is Psalm 119 (176 verses). It is a magnificent meditation celebrating the Word of God, which for the psalmist was the Torah (the Pentateuch, consisting of the first five books of the Old Testament). In verse 105, the psalmist declares, "Your word is a lamp to my feet and a light to my path." The Bible is just that: a light for guidance through this world and to the next. Only it, among all the ideas and religious texts of the world, can provide such guiding light. Theologian Carl F. H. Henry astutely addressed this truth, declaring, "Everywhere around us is strewn the philosophical wreckage of those who rely on the voice of conscience, on social utility, on aesthetic gratification, on majority consensus—on everything but a sure Word of God."[9] The Bible is that Word of God. It is an amazing book, and we should never underestimate its value, its claims, and its uniqueness. "God breathed it; men wrote it; we possess it."[10]

17. How does one deal with alleged errors and problem passages in the Bible?

There have been naysayers regarding the truthfulness of the Bible since the early centuries of the church. Various apologists for

Christianity such as Justin Martyr, Tertullian, Origen, and others have answered these skeptics in their writings. Interestingly, most of the kinds of arguments, and even specific arguments, that the early fathers dealt with have arisen in our day, though sometimes the arguments are dressed differently. The arguments posed against early Christianity usually related to the nature of Christ and alleged immoral activities of Christians, but some charged that the story of Jesus and records of that story were not true. The latter accusation is normal today and is the point of our interest. An added twist today is the assertion that the biblical accounts not only are fictional and not written by eyewitnesses, but also that the manuscripts are flawed, often intentionally altered by copyists.

The major contemporary attacks against the trustworthiness of the Bible among biblical scholars have come from members of the Jesus Seminar and Professor Bart Ehrman. We will address some of the charges from these two camps; then we will present the kinds of errors alleged by liberal scholars over the last couple of hundred years and provide answers to these claims.

First, however, we must frankly acknowledge that there are differences among accounts in the four gospels that must be dealt with, and there are problem passages in the Old and New Testaments in the areas of ethics, differing numbers in parallel accounts, and lack of historical evidence for some events and persons, among other things.

Nevertheless, the plethora of historical evidence for the persons, places, and events of the Bible should give confidence to the Christian who believes the Bible. We do not need to believe irrationally; we can have confidence that our faith in God and His Word is abundantly supported by archaeological and historical fact.

Scholars have already answered many of the alleged biblical errors of the past. For instance, the Bible mentions a great nation called the Hittites. During the Enlightenment until the late nineteenth century, critics of the Bible claimed that no such nation existed; if it did, they would have known. Then in 1876, the Hittites were discovered, along with thousands of clay tablets describing their lives, history, and commerce.

It is similarly alleged that the patriarchs of Genesis never existed, because outside of the Bible there is no historical proof for their lives. But this lack is to be expected. The patriarchs were largely nomads and unlikely to leave remains that would be found in the cities of the ancient world like Babylon, or even smaller ones such as Jericho.

It was claimed that Moses could not have written the Pentateuch; yet advanced writing abilities would certainly have been possessed by one "skilled in the wisdom of the Egyptians." Only if critics could prove that an Egyptian princess sometime between the fifteenth and thirteenth centuries B.C. did *not* rear Moses could such a charge be supported.

Supposedly the Bible exaggerates the reign of Solomon. Yet we have evidence of a highly civilized and thriving society from the tenth century at the chariot cities of Solomon at Megiddo, Gezer, and Hazor (1 Kings 9:15–19).

Regularly, the Bible is said to have a non-scientific worldview. But should one expect something different about any book written prior to the modern era? This does not mean that there is a contradiction between the Bible and genuine scientific facts. The Bible speaks in phenomenological language, as would be expected and just as we still do today. For instance, saying that the sun rises and sets does not imply that we believe the sun actually moves in respect to the earth (see chapter 15). The Genesis account of creation is not at variance with what we know to be true about science and is an explanation of God's creation in an orderly fashion and how He formed and filled the heavens and the earth. The list of objections goes on, but none of them has proved the Scriptures to be inaccurate.

The alleged errors in the Bible fall under several categories, namely, errors of numbers, genealogy, locations, conflicting accounts, incorrect references, history, quality of sources, and dating. We will provide examples of these and provide a brief response.[11]

Errors of Numbers

In several parallel passages in the Old Testament that describe the same incidents, the verses differ with each other. For example, English translations of 2 Samuel 10:18 say that David killed 700 charioteers and 40,000 horsemen, whereas 1 Chronicles 19:18 says that he killed 7,000 charioteers and 40,000 foot soldiers. Two issues arise here. First is the discrepancy between the 700 and 7,000, and the second relates to horsemen versus footmen. Both of these problems most likely relate to a copyist's errors in manuscript transmission rather than the biblical authors providing wrong information. It is difficult to know in this instance which is the more correct reading.

A second example is the age of King Jehoiachin when he began to reign. The book of 2 Chronicles 36:9 gives his age as eight, whereas 2 Kings 24:8 says he was eighteen. These numerals are very close in appearance in the Hebrew text and are likely transcription and transmission errors. Eighteen is most likely the correct original reading, since 2 Kings 24:8 says that Jehoiachin reigned only three months and, in the next verse (v. 9), that he did evil in the sight of Yahweh. It is unlikely that an eight-year-old would be acting in this manner.

One last example is easier to figure out than the preceding two. According to 1 Kings 4:26, Solomon had 40,000 stalls of horses for his chariots and 12,000 horsemen. But 1 Kings 10:26 indicates that he had 1,400 chariots. Assuming that this figure is correct, 4,000 stalls seems to be a more reasonable number than 40,000 stalls.

There is no evidence that the variances in any of the above numbers were in the original writings. They may easily have been made by a copyist. Making out numerals in Hebrew script, especially with faded or worn-out manuscripts, makes a copyist error more likely than that the discrepancy originated with the author of Kings or Chronicles.

Errors of Genealogy

Another charge of errors in the Bible concerns discrepancies in its genealogies. We will look at two of them, namely, the time span of Genesis 5 and 10 and the genealogies of Christ.

The genealogies of Scripture do not necessarily include every single descendant. This becomes abundantly clear with the practice of Matthew's use of a device called *gematria* in presenting the genealogy of Jesus. Matthew names fourteen generations of three sets which add up to the name David, fourteen being the numerical value of "dvd" (four plus six plus four) in Hebrew. Matthew used this device to emphasize that the Messiah was the son of David. Luke 3:36 omits one person who is found in Genesis 10:24 and the purpose of Luke's genealogy of Jesus is different than that of Matthew, and yet, reconciliation between the two genealogies is possible in a variety of ways.[12]

The difference between the genealogy of Jesus the Messiah in Matthew's gospel and Luke's gospel has never been a significant issue in church history. Both the church fathers and modern scholars have recognized that Matthew traces Jesus through David through the line that included Jeconiah (Coniah), whereas Luke traces Christ through David's son Nathan. The biblical text indicates that as a judgment from Yahweh, no descendant of Jeconiah would ever sit on David's throne (Jer. 22:30). Were Jesus to trace physically through that line to David, He could never be king of Israel. Instead, according to Luke, Jesus came physically by Mary through the line of Nathan to David, making Him truly the seed of David the king.

Similar to what we have demonstrated above, there is no reason why there cannot be lacunae in the genealogies of Genesis 5 and 10. Moreover, sometimes the "son" of someone was actually the grandson of that person, so that the word *son* did not indicate an immediate descendant. For example, Jesus is the Son of David, but not directly so.

Errors of Location

Confusion has sometimes arisen regarding the proper location for a particular act or event in the biblical narrative. For instance, many years ago the scholar Dewey Beegle sought to demonstrate that the biblical text was in error regarding the burial place of

Jacob. Beegle compared Genesis 23:19 and 50:13 with Stephen's words in Acts 7:16. But the supposed contradiction is caused by not carefully reading the text. The Genesis verses speak of the burial of Jacob, while Stephen, possibly relying on oral tradition, speaks of the burial of the sons of Jacob, not of Jacob himself.

Errors of Conflicting Accounts

It is customary among biblical skeptics[13] to point out seeming contradictions in parallel gospel accounts. The presence of angels at Jesus' tomb is a case in point. Matthew 28:2–5 and Mark 16:5 mention only one angel in the tomb, whereas Luke 24:4 and John 20:12 mention two. But the contradiction is superficial. There is no problem with two angels being at the site but an author focusing on only one because he is the more prominent one. One angel in particular rolled back the stone, frightened the guards, and began a conversation with the women. This one receives more notice in two of the accounts. Similar occasions occur regarding demons (Matt. 8:28 vs. Mark 5:2 and Luke 8:27) and blind men (Matt. 20:30 vs. Mark 10:46 and Luke 18:35). "One" is different from "one and only one."

The story of Peter's betrayal in Matthew 26:34, 74–75 and Luke 22:34, 60–61 differs with Mark's account in 14:30, 72. Because of this, some have suggested an error in the Bible. Observe the essence of the three accounts on the number of times that the rooster would crow and the number of denials:

> Matthew 26:34—"Before a rooster crows, you will deny Me three times."
> Luke 22:34—"The rooster will not crow today until you have denied three times that you know Me."
> Mark 14:30—"Before a rooster crows twice, you yourself will deny Me three times."

The argument for an error here is special pleading. Matthew and Luke are making a general statement about the crowing of the rooster, without special attention to detail. To them, the issue is the three denials. Mark, on the other hand, is Peter's gospel. He would have a vivid image of that night and how the crowing of the rooster held special significance for him. He is more detailed in giving the number of times that the rooster crowed because he actually heard it, and he is equally specific in the number of denials. The attempt by some (Cheney, *Life of Christ in Stereo*) to have six denials, three after each crowing, is unneeded. All that is needed is good, commonsense reading that accounts for the intention of the different gospel authors.

Errors of Incorrect Biblical References

Some skeptics expect believers in the Bible's trustworthiness to say, "Oops, that's wrong," regarding purportedly incorrect references. Supposedly, New Testament authors somehow quoted the wrong person. An example is Matthew's source for his reference to the Potter's Field (Matt. 27:9–10). Matthew gives a partial quotation from Zechariah 11:13, referring to the potter, but the primary sources for the Matthew passage that refers to the Potter's Field (cf. Matt. 27:6–9), not mentioned by Zechariah, are Jeremiah 19:2, 11 and 32:9. The common practice among writers of the New Testament, when blending quotations from or allusions to the Old Testament texts, was to connect the quotation to the more famous of the authors. Here Matthew refers to Jeremiah.

A similar example is found in Mark 1:2–3, in which Mark quotes from Malachi 3:1 and Isaiah 40:3, but attributes the statement only to Isaiah, the more prominent of the two prophets.

Errors of Quality of Sources

Some raise concerns of error in the Bible where the biblical authors quote from sources that are not part of the canonical text. Supposedly, such material is untrustworthy. But of course truth resides outside the Bible. For example, a person's name, age, parents' names, and other personal information don't have to appear in the Scriptures in order for them to be reliable. Any number of facts of history, science, math, and the like, are true in spite of their not being in the Bible.

When one speaks of the truthfulness of the Bible, he is saying that whatever an author of the Bible writes conforms to what is true about the statement. The Bible can truthfully record what evil people say, even if what they say is untruthful. For example, Satan lied to Adam and Eve. He was not truthful, but it is true that he said what he said. On the other hand, many things said by persons outside the Bible may also be truthful, and if the biblical authors quote them in order to prove the truthfulness of their arguments, then the sources were accurate and true.

We can give three examples of this, though there are more in the Old and New Testaments. In two instances, Jude quotes from two sources available to him in the first century A.D., namely, the Book of Enoch and the Assumption of Moses. In verses 14–15, Jude quotes the pseudepigraphical work Enoch, written in the intertestamental period: "Behold, the Lord came with many thousands of His holy ones, to execute judgment upon all, and to convict all the ungodly of all their ungodly deeds which they have done in an ungodly way, and of all the harsh things which ungodly sinners have spoken against Him." Though not everything in Enoch may be true, Jude affirms that this particular prophecy of the biblical Enoch, preserved from the earliest periods of human history and passed down through Moses, is accurate.

Likewise, in verse 9, Jude recounts the account of the controversy between Michael and Satan over the body of Moses. He says that Michael did not revile Satan but said, "The Lord rebuke you!" Michael actually said this, though one cannot have assurance that everything else in the Assumption of Moses is accurate.

The third example involves the quotes that the apostle Paul uses in addressing the philosophers in Acts 17. In verse 28, he quotes from the poem *Cretica* by the Cretan poet Epimenides, who said, "In him we live and move and have our being"; and, from *Phaenonlena* by the Cilician poet Aratus: "We are also his offspring."[14] In speaking of the Unknown God, Paul believed both of these statements to be true about the true and living God he proclaimed to the Athenians.

The work of the Holy Spirit through biblical authors ensures that they accurately quote their sources and guides them in the selection of source material.

Errors of Dating

Some skeptics who doubt the historicity of the Exodus of the Jews from Egypt claim that the length of a Hebrew sojourn in Egypt discussed in the Bible has conflicting time periods. Exodus 12:40 says that the children of Israel lived in Egypt for 430 years. Paul, in Galatians 3:17, says that the law given by Moses was given 430 years after the giving of the Abrahamic covenant. One scholar, Dewey Beegle, says that Abraham was seventy-five years old when he moved to Canaan and one hundred years old when Isaac was born. Isaac was sixty years old when Jacob was born, and Jacob was 130 years old when he went to Egypt. When one adds together twenty-five years, sixty years, and 130 years, the total is 215 years in Canaan. Since Exodus says that the children of Israel were in Egypt for 430 years, says Beegle, then the time from the giving of the covenant to Abraham to the giving of the law to Moses would be 645 years.[15]

Beegle errs in thinking that Paul's intent in mentioning 430 years was to trace the time of the law, in Exodus 20, to the giving of the covenant to Abraham in Genesis 12. Paul's point was that the law given to Moses was 430 years after the time of the patriarchs. The covenant was with Abraham, Isaac, and Jacob, not only with Abraham at its initiation in Genesis 12. The law does not invalidate this covenant with the patriarchs.

Principles to Use When Dealing with Alleged Errors in Scripture[16]	
Reason Why Biblical Critic Alleges Errors in Scripture	**Principle to Apply to Objection**
The solution for the biblical difficulty is not immediately explainable.	Simply because one cannot explain an event, or a literary text, does not mean that it is not explainable, only that the explanation is not yet available.
Multiple interpretations of a given biblical text cause a critic to believe that the text is faulty.	Even though a given literary text may be subject to a variety of interpretations, this in no way demonstrates that one of the interpretations may not be the correct one. This is also true in science and historical study, in which previous or alternate views have been discarded when better information is available. This does not mean that the text was wrong but that the interpreter did not have adequate information to make a proper judgment.
The critic does not carefully read the context of the passage in question so that the Scripture is viewed to be in error rather than the critic.	It is not uncommon to read biblical critics who allege that a biblical text is in error, when in reality the critic fails to read the passage carefully (so thinking there to be an error), or reads the text out of context.
The critic fails to interpret a difficult passage of Scripture in light of a given author's usage of terms and theology, or the broader biblical teaching on the topic.	Authors of the Bible use a variety of terms, sometimes doing so in light of the use of the terms or ideas in a given community to whom they write that is different from other authors of Scripture. Paul and James both use *faith*, but may have different nuances to the use of the word. Paul uses the term *spiritual* in Romans in a different way from how he uses the term in 1 Corinthians based on the difference of his discussions.
An obscure passage in which there is no consensus among scholars may be viewed as an error.	Some biblical passages are very difficult to understand, such as baptism for the dead in 1 Corinthians 15:29, but the difficulty is caused by our removal from the historical setting. This does not constitute an error in the Bible but a failure of our ability to understand it, and such passages should not be viewed as in conflict with clearer texts.

Because Scripture is written by humans with human limitations and capabilities, there is inevitable introduction of human error that should not be explained away.	Admittedly human beings used their knowledge and personalities in writing the Bible, but Scripture teaches that God superintended the process (2 Peter 1:20–21) to produce a book breathed out by God (2 Tim. 3:16).
Biblical texts present contradictory records with one Gospel having one person introduced while others have more than one.	The failure to mention the exact same information, such as angels present or persons healed (cf. Mark 5:1–20 and Luke 8:26–39), does not indicate error. When an author focuses on one angel or human, this does not deny the existence of the other. One does not mean only one. This is an example of incompleteness but not error.
The biblical authors, alleges the critic, improperly quote passages from the Old Testament, and so introduce errors into the New Testament text.	It is true that some of the New Testament quotations from the Old Testament are not identical with the Old Testament, but this arises based on whether the New Testament author is quoting from the Hebrew and Greek testaments, and also which version of them. This does not mean, however, that the New Testament author could not apply the specific Old Testament quotation to the theological point that he wishes to make.
The Bible approves of a number of erroneous statements and immoral practices, as seen by the recording of lies, murders, rape, incest, polygamy, and adultery.	The fact that a statement, an idea, or an act appears in the Bible does not mean that God promotes it. Rather, the Bible simply affirms that every event or statement is truthfully recorded. When the Serpent told Eve that she would not die, he was lying, but he did in fact say those words. Likewise, the Scripture tells of David's adultery with Bathsheba, but it does not condone his actions; rather, it provides a faithful record of David's sin.
The Bible is a pre-scientific book and so cannot be relied on in our scientific age. For example, the earth is not flat and the sun does not "rise."	The Bible speaks in phenomenological language, even as we do today. The "four corners of the earth" is an expression similar to the four points of the compass: north, south, east, and west. The sun does not actually rise, but it appears to, and the words sunrise and sunset are astronomical terms used today.

continued . . .

Principles to Use When Dealing with Alleged Errors in Scripture *continued*	
Reason Why Biblical Critic Alleges Errors in Scripture	**Principle to Apply to Objection**
Critics believe that the Bible is inaccurate in recording numbers, distances, and locations.	Exaggeration is a literary device that most people understand, and biblical authors use it. This is not a mistake. Moreover, associating larger cities for identification when a smaller, unfamiliar town is nearby was done by biblical authors for greater clarity and is not an error. These kinds of literary devices are used today and are not viewed as errors.
The many errors in the copying of the Hebrew and Greek texts make the idea of an errorless Scripture meaningless.	Certainly there are thousands of mistakes in copying among the many thousands of Hebrew and Greek manuscripts, not to mention ancient translations, but one can usually figure out the best reading by means of textual criticism. Moreover, when a doctrine may be questioned in a passage with questionable copying, the same doctrine is supported in another passage in which there is no question as to the proper reading of the manuscript.
General maxims in Scripture, such as are found in Proverbs or similar literature, are viewed as error.	Particularly proverbial literature is not giving absolutes or universal promises, but "rules of thumb" that may be practiced by the person who has wisdom, knowing when to use a particular wise saying and when to use an alternate maxim.

Conclusion

In concluding our answer to this question, we recommend the wise approach that St. Augustine describes in writing to Jerome:

> When perplexed by something in Scripture which appears to oppose the truth:
>
> Either the manuscript is faulty, or
> The translator has not caught the meaning of what was said, or
> I myself have failed to understand the meaning. (*Letter to Jerome* 82.3)

Were skeptics of Scripture as open to alternatives as Augustine, there would be far fewer criticisms of Scripture and far less embar-

rassment when history and archaeology support the texts that have
been disparaged.

18. Is the Bible God's final revelation?

Since the completion of the New Testament, several other books
have purported to be revelations from God. In the second century,
a number of spurious works, called pseudepigrapha, were supposedly written by apostles or cohorts of the apostles, such as Thomas,
Peter, Paul, and Barnabas. None of these has withstood scrutiny by
orthodox believers nor the test of time.

The major historical figure who claimed to be the new and true
prophet from God was Muhammad. Building on bits and pieces
of Judaism and Christianity, he alleged that Islam was the religion believed by the prophets of the Hebrew Bible and that Jesus
was a prophet from Allah who even spoke of Muhammad. All of
Muhammad's claims fall flat based on even rudimentary investigation, but his religion is held up by coercion rather than scholarship
or argument.

After Muhammad, and especially in the nineteenth century, several other people came forth claiming that they had new revelations
from God. Joseph Smith may be the most obvious and adventure-
some in his attempt to build a religion from an alleged revelation
from God, but there have been others such as Ellen White and,
later, Sun Myung Moon.

Last of all, there are those who claim today to be prophets and
apostles in the same vein as those of the first century. Although
they do not necessarily write down their thoughts as the Bible per
se, they claim to have revelations from God similar to the prophets
and apostles.

Why are the Old and New Testaments in fact the only true revelations from God, and why is the New Testament that we have
the complete and final revelation? To answer these questions,
let us clarify what is meant by the word *revelation*. We are *not*
speaking of being led by the Spirit of God or of having a sense

of specific, personalized guidance for our actions based on the wisdom we receive from reading the Bible. Rather, when we speak of revelation, we mean that God is unveiling something about Himself in order to advance His redemptive and kingdom program.

Jesus considered the Hebrew Scriptures to be the words, and the Word, of God—in part and in whole inspired. When He sought to deal with temptation, with false teaching, with controversy, and with how He should relate to God, His constant recourse was to the words of Holy Scripture. He found them fully authoritative and sufficient. Much of the new teaching that some people believed Jesus was presenting actually was from the Hebrew texts He had learned. He saw Himself as the fulfillment of the Hebrew Bible, but He never rejected its ongoing truthfulness relating to God, man, sin, salvation, the kingdom of God, and other essential doctrines.

The apostles dealt with Scripture in the same way. As Paul said, "All Scripture is breathed out by God, and profitable for teaching, for reproof, for correction, and for training in righteousness, so that the man of God may be complete, equipped for every good work" (2 Tim. 3:16–17 ESV). Personal revelations, new revelations, and new books from God are simply not needed. And though Paul is here speaking specifically of the Old Testament, the New Testament is similarly the inspired interpretation, explication, and clarification of God at work, embodied in the Messiah Jesus. As the writer of Hebrews says, "God, after He spoke long ago to the fathers in the prophets in many portions and in many ways, in these last days has spoken to us in His Son, whom He appointed heir of all things, through whom also He made the world" (Heb. 1:1). When John put the final touch to the last book of the New Testament, he put the capstone on God's revelation. Genesis begins with God as Creator of the heavens and earth, and Revelation ends with God as Creator of the new heavens and new earth. Genesis begins with human failure, sin, and sorrow, and with Satan trying to spoil the plans of God, while Revelation ends with the final redemption of mankind and the banishment of sin, sorrow, and Satan from the renewed creation of God. There is simply no more that needs to be said to tell us about who God is and what His plan is, either for the universe in general or us in particular.

19. How did Jesus and the apostles view the Bible?

Jesus and the apostles understood that their Jewish Scriptures—the same as the thirty-nine books in the Protestant Old Testament, though ordered and numbered differently—were authoritative and divinely inspired. Jesus confirmed the authority of the Old Testament and promised the New Testament.[17] Old Testament scholar Walter C. Kaiser Jr. writes:

> There can be little doubt that Jesus pointed to the books held in reverence by the Jews of his earthly pilgrimage and pointedly said: "These are the Scriptures that testify about me" (Jn. 5:39). And if it be asked just what was the scope of the books held in esteem as inspired and canonical at that time, the answer is found in Matthew 23:35 and its parallel text in Luke 11:51. There, Jesus showed the sweep of the canon as he knew it to be the same twenty-four books that are the present English thirty-nine.[18]

When one reads the four gospel accounts of the life and ministry of Jesus Christ, the following are among the teachings of Jesus about the content of the books of the Old Testament:

- Jesus said that the Old Testament, in whole and in part, had divine authority (Matt. 4:4, 7, 10; 5:27; 19:4–5; 22:29, 43; 24:15; Luke 16:16; 17:27).
- Jesus called the Scriptures the Word of God (John 10:35).
- Jesus declared the authors of Scripture were directed by God in the writing of them (Mark 12:36; Matt. 24:15).

- Jesus confirmed persons and miracles of the Old Testament
  as true, among them
    Isaiah (Mark 7:6)
    Moses (Mark 7:10)
    Abel (Luke 11:51)
    Adam and Eve (Matt. 19:4–5)
    Noah and the flood (Matt. 24:37–39)
    Sodom and Gomorrah (Luke 10:12)
    Jonah and the fish (Matt. 12:39–41)
- Jesus verified the absolute trustworthiness of the Scripture
  (Luke 16:17).
- Jesus promised that he would preserve His message through
  the apostles (John 14:25–26; 16:13).

The apostles and other New Testament writers also had a high
view of Scripture.[19]

- The apostles viewed their authority and writing as coming
  from God (Rom. 1:1, 5; 1 Cor. 14:37; Gal. 1:8–9; 1 Thess. 2:13;
  1 Tim. 2:7).
- The apostles affirmed the people and events recorded in the
  Old Testament, such as
    Creation (Col. 1:16)
    Adam and Eve (1 Tim. 2:13–14)
    Sacrifices of Abel and Cain (Heb. 11:4)
    Rapture of Enoch (Heb. 11:5)
    Tithes to Melchizedek (Heb. 7:1–3)
    Ishmael (Gal. 4:21–26)
    Exodus through the Red Sea (1 Cor. 10:1–2)
    Provision of water and manna in the wilderness (1 Cor.
      10:3–5)
    Fall of Jericho (Heb. 11:30)
    Miracles of Elijah (James 5:17–18)
    Daniel in the lions' den (Heb. 11:33)

- Paul's writings are specifically called Scripture (2 Peter 3:15–16).
- Paul quotes Deuteronomy and Luke together as Scripture (1 Tim. 5:18 citing Deut. 25:4 and Luke 10:7).

Jesus and the apostles knew that the Old Testament Scriptures they used were the inspired Word of God, and they also knew that what they wrote was divinely inspired. Jesus promised He would preserve His message through the apostles (John 14:25–26; 16:13) and He empowered them to continue His work and preach His message (Acts 2:1–4; Matt. 16:19). They did so, and their teaching served as the foundation for the beliefs of Christianity and the early church (Eph. 2:20; Acts 2:42 and Acts 15).

20. Is there extrabiblical support for the reliability of the biblical accounts?

Very little of the ancient world has been excavated, considering the available sites that could be, and even though we have thousands of ancient documents written on clay, stone, papyrus, and animal skins, these are a small fraction of the total initially produced. Moreover, ancient writings of the ancient Near East and Graeco-Roman world were primarily concerned with their own history and ideas. Only at times do the interests of ancient cultures and the people, events, customs, and ideas of the Bible coincide. When they do, however, the biblical material has been shown to be a trustworthy historical record. Some critics have desired to undermine the plethora of data in the Bible, but as "archaeology catches up with the Bible," the biblical text fares well.

Before determining whether there is acceptable extrabiblical support for the Bible's reliability, one must understand the nature of historical investigation. There are only two ways to acquire knowledge, namely, by direct experience or by receiving that knowledge from someone else. Historical investigation necessarily relies on the written or spoken account of someone's personal experience or on that person's records of other people's experience. Another way of saying it is, our documents of history are secondhand. This does not mean, however, that they are unreliable, either in part or as a whole. One might think that the passage of time might render ancient documents, even the Bible, untrustworthy, but this is faulty thinking. It is irrelevant whether a document we are studying is five years old or 5,000 years old. Its credibility relates rather to how far removed the written document is from the events and words that it records. For example, if Matthew's gospel was written a hundred years after the events, persons, and words it speaks of, then it has limited reliability (unless its sources were the words or writings of eyewitnesses). But if the author of the gospel of Matthew was an eyewitness or had information given to him by an eyewitness, then its reliability increases dramatically. Luke is an example of someone who was known not to be an eyewitness of facts found in his gospel; yet his careful research of sources, first- and secondhand, of those who were eyewitnesses has been established repeatedly, and his firsthand personal accounts in Acts are considered a model of historical factuality. The Bible contains eyewitness accounts as well as reliable use of secondhand accounts and both support the trustworthiness of the Bible.

All of this discussion thus far speaks to the matter of intrinsic credibility of ancient sources. But what about fragmentary records and the interpreter's personal bias in doing research? All contemporary and historical books are limited in scope and fragmentary in presentation. It cannot be otherwise. An author cannot possibly research or include everything that could be said, or a book could never be written nor read. It would simply be too unmanageable. Consequently, an author or speaker focuses on the points and data that are particularly pertinent to his or her purposes. One does not need to know everything to know something. This is a fact of research and a fact of life. What we do know about the statements of Scripture is that, when they are tested against the limited information that we have from the ancient world, they prove true.

The stories of the patriarchs are consistent with what we know of the culture and life of the nomadic peoples of the ancient Near East, and even though we find no direct evidence of biblical characters such as Noah or Abraham, one must have credible reasons to reject the biblical text in these matters. The sands of the Sinai do not reveal the traces of a people wandering in the desert, and it is unreasonable to demand that they should. Only had such people built cities and created permanent dwellings would any detectable evidence of their lives remain, based on the kinds of finds that archaeologists make.

Moreover, though the records of Egypt have little to say of a large group of Hebrews leaving Egypt after their God devastated Egypt, one would not expect public announcements of such things. However, the tombs of Egypt may offer some indication that there were plagues, and also that Egyptian soldiers drowned in the Red Sea. These are highly debatable and may be interpreted differently by scholars; however, one of the authors has seen Egyptian paintings of the parting of the Red Sea and floating Egyptian corpses which may lend support. Recent evidence on a stele in Egypt may also reveal that the Hebrew people were already within the land of Canaan 200 years earlier than previously thought, around 1400 B.C. This is consistent with the early view of the Exodus occurring in 1446 B.C.[20]

Archaeological discoveries in Israel in recent years have uncovered the historicity of kings such as Uzziah, David, Jeroboam, and several other persons involved in royal service and the building of the first temple. As well, the physical landscape of the mountains, valleys, rivers, and towns of the Old Testament have been identified and are consistent with the biblical account.

This is also true of the New Testament regarding biblical sites and geography as well as persons like Pilate, Herod the Great, the Herodian family, and even James, the brother of Jesus. All are known through historical documents and archaeological finds. Significantly, the existence of Jesus, including his works and death, have been supported in a number of documents in the Graeco-Roman world by people such as Josephus, Pliny the Younger, Suetonius, Tacitus, and Lucian. The events, places, and officials recorded by Luke have been found to be highly accurate, despite attempts by scholars several decades ago to discount the books as not credible and fictionalized.[21]

Following are a few of the comments made by several Old and New Testament scholars, both liberal and conservative, about the reliability of the Bible:

> Sir Fredrick Kenyon: "The interval then between the dates of original composition and the earliest extant evidence becomes so small as to be in fact negligible, and the last foundation for any doubt that the Scriptures have come down to us substantially as they were written has now been removed. Both the authenticity and the general integrity of the books of the New Testament may be regarded as finally established."[22]

> A. N. Sherwin-White: "For Acts the confirmation of historicity is overwhelming. Yet Acts is, in simple terms and judged externally, no less of a propaganda narrative than the Gospels, liable to similar distortions. But any attempt to reject its basic historicity even in matters of detail must now appear absurd. Roman historians have long taken it for granted."[23]

> Nelson Glueck: "It may be stated categorically that no archaeological discovery has ever controverted a biblical reference. Scores of archaeological findings have been made which confirm in clear outline or exact detail historical statements in the Bible."[24]

> Sir William Ramsey: "Luke is a historian of the first rank; not merely are his statements of fact trustworthy . . . [but]

this author should be placed along with the very greatest of historians."[25]

William F. Albright: "Aside from a few die-hards among older scholars, there is scarcely a single biblical historian who has not been impressed by the rapid accumulation of data supporting the substantial historicity of the Patriarchal tradition."[26]

Edwin M. Yamauchi: "Until the breakthrough of archaeological discoveries, the stories about the biblical patriarchs—Abraham, Isaac, and Jacob—were subject to considerable skepticism. . . . In the last thirty years, however, a steadily increasing flow of materials from Mesopotamia and Syria-Palestine—from Mari, from Nuzi, from Alalakh—has convinced all except a few holdovers of the authenticity of the patriarchal narratives."[27]

The Bible presents itself as a reliable guide for faith and life. Its prophets repeatedly declared their words to be the very word of God; the apostle Paul stated that all Scripture comes from the breath of God; and the trustworthiness of these biblical claims is borne out in the crucible of objective scholarship as scholars have uncovered the source materials in the ancient world that confirm the Bible's reliability.[28]

PART 4

The Gospels and Acts

21. How reliable are the historical accounts in the Gospels and the book of Acts?

Can we trust the records given to us in the Gospels and Acts? Throughout church history until the critical period that followed the Enlightenment, few questioned whether the life of Jesus presented in the four gospels and the events of the early church given in the book of Acts were authentic and trustworthy accounts. Currently, it is common among critical biblical scholars to doubt many events in the life of Jesus and the apostles, especially any with miraculous elements. Part of their reason for this lies in at least two presuppositions. One, the accounts were not written by actual eyewitnesses or even disciples of eyewitnesses, but by anonymous persons living in the later decades of the first century A.D., perhaps even the early second century. Second, critics presuppose that any account of a supernatural act of God is nothing more than fictional exaggeration designed to give credence to Jesus or one of His apostles or to strengthen the author's rendition of events. A third, less problematic objection, and an inaccurate one, is that the authors' motive is to teach theology in their books rather than present factual history.

Are the Gospels and Acts theology, or are they history? We maintain that they are both. The writers of the Gospels wrote historical accounts of Jesus' words, works, and life events that proclaim Him, theologically, to be the Promised One from God foretold in the Jewish Scriptures. In view of the theological element, some scholars in critical circles believe that the events recorded in the Gospels and Acts, especially the miracles of Jesus, never really happened. Supposedly, these books mold history to fit the theological theme that the authors are setting forth.

Whether one is speaking of the Gospels or Acts or any other work of history, certain things are true. All historians have the same limitations of historical facts and events. Much of history is not observable, so that the historian must rely on his sources of people who experienced the history. In so doing, the historian must determine the trustworthiness of the stories. Historians must deal with fragmented accounts as well as their own biases; but they must not be jaded, nonfactual, or deceptive in their writing. The veracity of an account depends on the truthfulness and diligence of its author. Though it is often claimed that the authors of the gospel texts were not eyewitnesses or even disciples of eyewitnesses, there is no serious evidence to support this charge. The critics who make such claims harbor a number of undisclosed presuppositions.[1] But those who were much closer to the time of the writing believed that Matthew, Mark, Luke, and John wrote the Gospels and that Luke wrote Acts. No substantive facts have ever contravened this truth.

Regarding the book of Acts, Luke provides a carefully laid-out presentation of what transpired following his Gospel, and he did so in a largely chronological manner. After joining Paul in Troas, Luke begins to use the word *we* throughout much of the remainder of the text (Acts 16:10–17; 20:5–21:18; 27:1–28:16), when he was an eyewitness of the events and words that transpired. Scholars have generally acknowledged that Luke's representations of persons, cities, terms, and the like throughout Acts are substantiated as new historical and archaeological evidence is found. The book presents thirty-two countries, fifty-four cities, and nine islands of the Mediterranean, and it spans about thirty years.[2]

There are a variety of sources behind Acts. For instance, when

Luke was at Antioch, a copy of the decrees of the apostolic council in Jerusalem (Acts 21:25) would likely have been available for him to consult in writing Acts 15; or, alternatively, he may have found the decrees in the archives at the Jerusalem church. Luke's association with Paul could have provided information regarding the earlier life of Paul when he was still persecuting the church. The list goes on.

However, much as he is an exacting historian, Luke is also a theologian; he sees the movement of God behind history. He recognizes the work of God in establishing the church on the day of Pentecost. He sees how the thousands of converts from Jerusalem to Rome are a fulfillment of Jesus' words that the gospel would spread throughout the whole world (Acts 1). Luke believes that the Holy Spirit is active in the church and that the church is following the will of God in proclaiming Jesus. Nothing in this requires Luke to invent stories or tell lies.

One further issue remains: What about the reliability of these New Testament books that are about 2,000 years old? Can we trust such ancient documents, which are removed so far from our personal experience? One might think that the enormous time between the writing of the historical records and today would bring into question the accuracy of the events related in the Gospels and Acts. But this line of thinking is incorrect; how much time has passed is irrelevant to the historical trustworthiness of those accounts. What *is* relevant is the time between when the words and events recorded in them actually occurred and the time when they were set in writing by the authors. Considering that the Gospels and Acts are written within a single generation of the persons and events represented in the books, any inaccuracies or falsehoods would have been challenged and corrected by those who were their contemporaries. But this never happened.[3]

The Credibility of Historical Events Determined by Temporal Proximity to the Record of the Event

22. How reliable is eyewitness testimony?

The reliability of eyewitness testimony can vary according to a number of factors. Is one speaking of what one sees or hears? Are the events or words heard over a prolonged period of time or in passing? Does the value of eyewitness testimony vary with given cultures? Or with the difference in time between when an event is observed and when it is recorded? Let us examine these questions.

In contemporary Western society, much emphasis is placed on having easy access to recorded information and as a result, many people are not adept at remembering what they hear or read. This was not true in the times of the Bible, particularly the New Testament. It was customary for disciples of rabbis, and the Jews in general, to memorize volumes of information that could be transmitted to future generations. One is reminded of the movie by Ray Bradbury, *Fahrenheit 451*, in which books were forbidden, so that individuals would memorize books to pass along to others. Birger Gehardsson has demonstrated in his book *Memory and Manuscript* that such capacity was not unusual in the ancient world. Such is also the case in less technological societies in the Middle East, where Muslims memorize the Qur'an.

In our society, we are not dependent on memory and so have become somewhat lazy mentally. This was made clear to one of the authors years ago when he started the study of Greek. After being required to memorize hundreds of Greek words and paradigms, he soon began to quickly memorize everything that he set his mind to.

The quality of eyewitness testimony varies greatly.[4] It depends on whether a person is exposed to a person, event, or speech for a short or long period of time. For example, if a person you were not paying attention to walked past you, you might not be able to identify that person accurately if asked to, and your identification would be suspect in a police lineup. On the other hand, if you were asked to identify someone whom you had been exposed to repeatedly, or if you were to recount a teaching that you had heard a number of times, your testimony would be of a higher quality and greater value. The apostles John and Peter emphasize the level of contact that the disciples had with Jesus. John says that the Logos dwelt among them and they beheld His glory (John 1:14). In 1 John 1:1–3, John describes the nature of their eyewitness. They heard the Logos with their own ears, saw Him with their eyes, and even touched Him with their hands. This was no cursory meeting; it was a long engagement. Thus their testimony was true. Peter said that the apostles had not invented myths but were eyewitnesses of the majesty of Jesus (2 Peter 1:16–18).

Last of all, the events spoken about in the Gospels occurred mostly during a three-year period during which the disciples had daily contact with Jesus. They heard Him give the same teaching a number of times and saw the results of His miracles. This happened from approximately A.D. 30–33. Within twenty to thirty years, the first three gospels were penned. John's gospel was within fifty years. We should also suppose that the accounts were carefully repeated again and again and were subject to correction by a number of other eyewitnesses. This was not the so-called "telephone game" in which a brief message gets mangled as it passes from one hearer to the next in a chain. It was no game and was not distorted. The disciples took seriously what was spoken by their Teacher, and thanks to their ongoing exposure to Him, He had ample opportunity to ensure that they understood Him correctly. They remembered what they had seen and heard until the time when it was set in writing. Moreover, as Robert Gundry demonstrates in his dissertation *The Use of the Old Testament in St. Matthew's Gospel*, it was not uncommon for disciples to take notes of their teacher's lessons. Matthew could have used such notes later in composing his gospel.[5]

23. What kind of literature is a gospel?

The first four books of the New Testament are called gospels, but few Christians are aware just what the term *gospel* actually means. The word is a transliteration of two Old English words, *god spel*, meaning "good news." The Old English derives, in turn, from the Greek word *euangelion*, which is also a combination of two words, *eu* and *angelos*, meaning, once again, "good news." In reality, there is only one gospel, or good news: that in the person of Jesus, God came among humanity as a human to seek and save through His death and resurrection those who place their trust in Him. However, we have four authors who developed four complementary ways to understand Jesus and His mission. Likewise, the question of what the Gospels are in literary terms may be answered four different ways. Three tell what the Gospels are not, and one tells what they are.

A gospel is not a biography. A biography is concerned with information about a person in regard to his or her background, culture, environment, and psychological makeup. Were the four accounts of Jesus a biography, we would expect much information about His early life, His interests, His brother and sisters, His mother and father, and His family's impact on His development. A biography would go into much more detail about other matters beside His ministry and final days.

A gospel is not an Acts. These kinds of works were concerned with narrative of heroic deeds by a notable person. We see this partially in the Gospels, but there is little content that focuses on these matters.

A gospel is not a memoir. Memoirs are concerned with the sayings of a famous person, but this is only part of what we find in the Gospels.

A gospel is an entirely new genre of literature. It is primarily concerned with the preaching material (*kerygma*) of the early church—i.e. those areas concerned with the saving Messiah, the substance of the good news. We receive glimpses of biography, acts, and memoir, but the primary focus of all of these matters is to provide a picture of Jesus as the one in whom we may put our trust to be saved. As Ralph Martin says, "These books were preaching materials, designed to tell the story of God's saving action in the life, ministry, death, and resurrection of Jesus of Nazareth. They were called Gospels because they gave the substance of *the gospel*, declared in Romans 1:16 to be God's power to salvation to all who believe."[6]

24. What is the Synoptic problem?

In reading the four gospels, Matthew, Mark, Luke, and John, you soon become aware that they share many of the same discourses and events in the life of Jesus. As well, they have many other stories that are unique to a specific gospel. Study of the gospels, particularly Matthew, Mark, and Luke, is called Synoptic studies. The term *synoptic* comes from two Greek words: *syn*, meaning "together," and *optic*, meaning "see." Thus, when one views the Gospels side by side instead of harmonizing them into one account, you are doing what a synoptic scholar does. The Synoptic problem deals with why these accounts share some of the same material while other material is unique. John is treated separately since it contains only 2 percent of the material found in the other three gospels.

Some scholars have argued an interdependence theory in which the first author wrote his account, probably from oral tradition. Then the second author used the first account and added his own material. Lastly, the third author used both accounts, compiling them with his own material. Different scholars have ascribed all three of these positions to each of the first three gospels. But the theory has difficulty explaining the difference in order in these gospels, or why the later authors omitted portions of the former works.

A second view is that there was an original gospel (*urevangelium*) from which the authors of the Gospels drew their material, probably in Aramaic. This theory is based on a statement by the church father Papias that Matthew's gospel was written in Hebrew. The shared content supposedly comes from the Aramaic, whereas the portions that differ come from later material developed after the Aramaic had been written. This view offers no explanation for the absence of the original gospel or the sources used in writing it, nor does it tell why there are omissions of purportedly available materials.

A third perspective is that there were a number of fragments of the words and works of Jesus which served as the original sources that gave rise to the existing Gospels. Where the Gospels agree, supposedly the same fragments were used, and in the places where they vary, other fragments were used.

A theory similar to the fragmentary view above is form criticism. Form critics attempt to understand how the different segments of the gospel books came together. According to form critics, different stories and sayings came together gradually over the years following Christ's death, generally in oral form, and were eventually compiled into a book. These stories are viewed with suspicion and supposedly contain myth and exaggeration.

Another view says that the passing down of oral tradition was common in the ancient world. Thus, cohesive stories and sayings of Jesus were transmitted verbally by eyewitnesses and those who heard them until finally the spoken accounts were written down into what we know as the Gospels. This view is probably true to some extent, but it does not explain the differences that exist between the three gospels, or the different perspectives they reflect among the authors.

Still other scholars maintain that the authors either were eyewitnesses of the events and words of Jesus, or else they depended on eyewitnesses. Either way, they wrote down what they knew or had learned from eyewitnesses, but they used this common material to give a personal and intentional development to the various aspects of the life of Jesus. Matthew developed the life of Christ to present Him as the kingly Messiah. Mark, sharing Peter's recollection, presented Jesus as the servant of Yahweh, the Messiah who came to seek and to save the lost.

Contemporary scholars, both liberal and conservative, have tended to believe that Mark was the first gospel, though prior to the critical period of the last 200 years, Matthew was viewed as the first gospel. Which position a person adopts is not necessarily a matter of orthodoxy. Good arguments can be made for each of the Synoptic Gospels to have been the written first. The majority position has been graphed below.

Suggested Relationships of the Synoptic Gospels and Their Sources

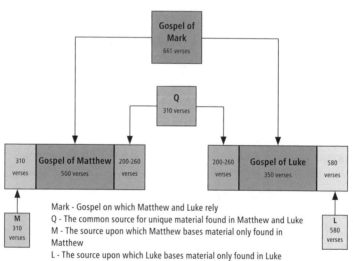

Mark - Gospel on which Matthew and Luke rely
Q - The common source for unique material found in Matthew and Luke
M - The source upon which Matthew bases material only found in Matthew
L - The source upon which Luke bases material only found in Luke

This chart assumes the majority view that Mark was the first Gospel and was relied upon by Matthew and Luke.

PART 5

The Canonicity
of the Bible

25. Who determined which books to put in the Bible?

No one human being decided which books would be part of the collection that makes up the Bible. It is likely that some of the books that were written and read by the people of God were not even viewed as Scripture from God at the time. However, the authority of the prophets and apostles began to be recognized over time by the recipients, and the works were preserved for the next generation.

Other books, however, were seen as God's Words from their initiation. Old Testament figures recognized by the Israelites as true prophets of God wrote their oracles and predictions of blessing and judgment. The proclamation, "Thus says Yahweh," appeared so often that the prophets' writings were viewed as inspired and were preserved. Other sources of history (cf. 1 Chron. 29:29; 2 Chron. 9:29; Esther 2:23; 10:2) and prophecy existed in the days of the prophets, but these have not been preserved for us.

Similarly, the New Testament's writings rang with the authority that Christ gave His apostles before He ascended to the Father. Paul stated to the Corinthians that the words he spoke to them were the commands of God.

In the New Testament period, only four gospels were written, and as they gradually passed around the churches of the Roman Empire, they were viewed as inspired. The New Testament letters are a different story. By the second century, the entire church embraced most of the letters of Paul, John, James, and Peter as authoritative and inspired. There were, however, exceptions. For instance, the apostolic origins of 2 Peter and Revelation were initially questioned. Not until the third and fourth centuries did these writings find universal acceptance by the churches, along with Hebrews and a few other books.

With the above background in place, we can now answer the question of who determined which books to put in the Bible. First of all, God did, for He inspired the Scriptures through the prophets and apostles. Second, humans did. Early Christians were not naive. They carefully scrutinized the biblical books to determine whether God had in fact inspired them and whether they were indeed written by the persons who claimed, or were considered by others, to be their authors.

By the time of Jesus, the entire twenty-two books of the Jewish Old Testament were embraced by the Jewish people, and by the fourth century there was universal acceptance of the twenty-seven books of our current New Testament. Other books for the Jews, and later for Gentile Christians, were helpful in providing a historical understanding and for their devotional value, and these books are accepted by the Roman Catholic and Eastern Orthodox Church. But only our current Bible of sixty-six books qualifies as the Word of God.

26. What criteria were used to include or exclude a book from the Bible?

Scripture teaches that the books of the Bible are divinely inspired by God (2 Tim. 3:16; 2 Peter 1:20–21) and were canonical from the moment they were written. They were inspired before they were recognized as being canonical; it was not canonization that gave them inspiration. The inclusion or exclusion of a book was not a determination made by individuals, groups, councils, or institutions, but was a progressive discovery and recognition of which books God had inspired. There was a cause-and-effect relationship between inspiration and canonization: inspiration of the writing by God caused it to be placed in the canon of Scripture. Historically, the compilation of the books of the New Testament came as members of the early church, guided by the Holy Spirit, recognized the authority of the different books, following the example of the Jews with respect to the Old Testament. Though all inspired books were canonical in quality from the moment of their writing, they were not totally acknowledged as such by the early church. The completed canon was finally and formally certified at the Council of Carthage in A.D. 397.

With respect to the Old Testament, books recognized as canonical were written during the prophetic period from Moses to Artaxerxes (ca. 1400–400 B.C.). They were written by individuals directed by God, showed evidence of being God-breathed, and were recognized as such by the people of God. There are numerous examples of recognition and acceptance of Old Testament books within the passages of Scripture. For example, the writings of Moses were immediately accepted as the authoritative words of God (Exod. 24:3) and are cited throughout the Old Testament. We read also that Joshua's words were written "in the book of the law" (Josh. 24:26), and we read that Jesus considered the Old Testament authoritative and consequently canonical (Luke 24:44; John 10:35). The New Testament writers also taught the inspiration of the Old Testament and indicated its authoritativeness by citing parts of it.

One group of books that has been accepted by some and rejected by others through the centuries is the Apocrypha. These books, sometimes numbered at fourteen and sometimes at fifteen depending on their grouping, were deemed canonical by the Roman

Catholic Church at the Council of Trent (1545–63) and also initially appeared in Protestant Bibles under a separate section before being dropped for containing teachings that were viewed by Protestants as unbiblical (e.g., prayers for the dead, as in 2 Maccabees 12:45–46, and salvation by works, as in Tobit 12:9).[1]

The books of the Apocrypha were written between 200 B.C. and A.D. 100 and describe with considerable accuracy the religious, political, and social conditions of the years between the Old and New Testaments, although there are historical and doctrinal errors. However, no Hebrew canon of the Old Testament contains these books, and they were not received as Scripture by Jews in Jesus' day. Additionally, Christ and the New Testament writers never cite from the Apocrypha, yet they cited liberally from the Old Testament. With minor exceptions, all lists of canonical books in the first four centuries A.D. exclude these books. Finally, these books make no claim for inspiration or to be the work of a prophet.

A second group of books surrounding the Old Testament but rejected by everyone is called the *pseudepigrapha* (literally "false inscriptions"). This is the name given to a large group of Jewish writings produced between 200 B.C. and A.D. 200. Some of these books claim to have been written by Adam, Enoch, Moses, and Ezra and include works such as the Book of Adam and Eve, the Martyrdom of Isaiah, the Assumption of Moses, 1 and 2 Enoch, and the Sibylline Oracle. In addition to false claims of authorship, they have fanciful content and some outright false doctrinal teachings. They were never included in the canon of Scripture.

Even though the New Testament authors reference some of these books (e.g., Book of Enoch 1:9 and the Assumption of Moses 1:9 in Jude 14–15), the writings are not canonical. The fact that the New Testament authors cite from them argues not for their canonicity, but for the truthfulness of the statement cited. Just as the writers of the New Testament can cite the pagan poets Aratus (Acts 17:28), Meander (1 Cor. 15:33), and Epimenides (Titus 1:12), so too can they cite from the pseudepigrapha.[2]

With respect to New Testament books recognized as canonical, an apostle authored each writing, or one closely associated with an apostle and showing evidence that it was inspired. There had to be *apostolicity.* Further, each writing's content needed to be spiritual in nature and agree with the teachings of the apostles; thus, it needed to show *orthodoxy.* Writings that were contradictory to what the apostles taught or to what was taught in the Old Testament were not recognized as canonical. There was also a criterion of *catholicity*, or universal recognition of the book. Was the book widely used in the churches?

To be recognized as canonical, a writing had to meet each of the above three criteria.[3] Thus, for example the early writing Shepherd of Hermas did not gain acceptance because of the uncertainty of its authorship, even though it was widely used and read.

Biblical support for acceptance of the New Testament canon can be found in several scriptural references. For example, Peter associated the writings of Paul as Scripture (2 Peter 3:15–16); Paul may have cited Luke in 1 Timothy 5:18 (cf. Luke 10:7); and the writings of the New Testament were read publicly in the churches along with the Old Testament (1 Thess. 5:27; Col. 4:16; Rev. 1:3; 1 Tim. 4:13). With respect to apostolicity, we find that apostolic authority was promised through Christ (John 16:12–15) and recognized by the early church (Acts 2:42; Eph. 2:20). Concerning recognition by the early church, we read that Luke wrote his gospel in order that the exact truth of Jesus' life might be known (Luke 1:1–4), dispelling false ideas about Jesus' life. Similarly, Paul warned the Thessalonian believers of a false letter then in circulation (2 Thess. 2:2). Apostolic authority and writing was known and recognized.

As with the Old Testament, there were writings excluded from the New Testament canon. In the first century, almost 300 non-canonical writings relating to the church were produced, but these writings were often heretical and fanciful. They did not meet the tests of canonicity and were never accepted into the canon.

27. Could more books properly be added to the Bible today?

The current Bible that we possess was composed by prophets of God in the Old Testament times and apostles of Christ in New Testament times. These were necessary requirements for the authority of these books. The prophets were the very mouthpieces of God and spoke the words of God. These words were revelations of God's mind for the people of God. Similarly, the apostles of the New Testament were given the responsibility to communicate, through the Holy Spirit, whatever Jesus had taught (John 14:26), with the promise that the Spirit of truth would lead them into all truth (John 16:13). Peter tells us that holy men of God were carried along by the Holy Spirit in declaring the Word of God (2 Peter 1:21).

With respect to the authors of the New Testament books, there was an absolute requirement of being a witness of Christ's resurrection or writing as a surrogate for one who was a witness, as in the case of John Mark for Peter and Luke for Paul. For the twelve disciples, in specific, this was necessary because they were to communicate the words and works of Jesus in His ministry; they had to be with Him from the baptism of John through the resurrection (Acts 1:21–22). Paul was a witness of the resurrected Lord, but he had no personal knowledge of Jesus' earthly ministry, something that was not required of him since he did not write a gospel.

In view of the above, no book could be added by a contemporary author to the sixty-six books we now possess. But what if another book from Old Testament times or New Testament times were to be found that was written by a biblical prophet or apostle? We know that Paul wrote other letters, so what if one of these were discovered? This would be an unlikely scenario, since the church of the early centuries would already have had access to those letters, but the fathers of the early church never speak of any. It is highly doubtful that they would be found; being written on papyrus and not preserved by the church, they would have perished long ago.

Moreover, even if we did find such books, we would have no way of determining whether they were genuine.

28. Why do the Roman Catholic, Eastern Orthodox, and Protestant Bibles have different books, and what are they?

The variations in the number of books accepted as biblical by the three major groups of Christians (Protestant, Roman Catholic, and Orthodox) are based not on the books of the New Testament, but on the number of books of the Old Testament that each group accepts. Protestants accept thirty-nine books, Roman Catholics accept forty-six, and Orthodox Christians accept fifty-one (with different titles for some of the books). The variation arises from the acceptance or rejection of the Apocrypha and from differences between Roman Catholicism and Orthodoxy regarding the number of books in the Apocrypha.

29. What does the phrase "Canon of the Bible" mean?

Canon is originally a Greek word meaning "rule" or "standard of measure," such as a reed or rod. As the word came to be used in the early church, it had a twofold meaning: first, a concrete and definite decision, such as a decree from a church synod or council that set a binding norm of belief or practice; and, second, a list, index, or table.[4] This second meaning is the one normally applied to the Bible from the third or fourth century A.D. through today. Usage of the word means either the list of books deemed authoritative that comprises the totality of the Bible, or the list of books in each of the two Testaments—that is, the canon of the Old Testament and the canon of the New Testament.

Over time, users came to understand the list of books as equivalent to their contents, such that the two were functionally identical in communication. In the same way, we might say, "I bought the grocery list and put it in the refrigerator," meaning that we purchased all of the items on the list and put them away. Similarly, canon came to mean not only the list but also the entirety of its contents.

30. When was the canonization of the Old Testament completed?

The dating of the close of the Old Testament canon is marked by presuppositions, disagreement, and confusion. Our view, following that of David Noel Freedman, Walter C. Kaiser Jr., and others, is that the canonization was complete by 400–350 B.C.[5] Old Testament scholar David Noel Freedman writes, "The major components of the Hebrew Bible in substantially the form in which they have come down to us were organized and compiled, published and promulgated during the Babylonian Exile [587–510 B.C.]."[6]

Other scholars argue that the canon remained open until later in Jewish history, at least among some Jewish groups such as those at Qumran.[7] At the time of the writing of the New Testament books during the first century, the thirty-nine books of the Old Testament were accepted as Scripture. At the latest, the canon of the Old Testament was completed in the first century A.D.; however, no official and formally accepted standard Hebrew Scripture existed for wide use by the Jewish communities until the development of the Masoretic Text. This text was developed from the sixth through eleventh centuries, mostly in the tenth century, and was published after the advent of the printing press. It appeared first in the Bomberg rabbinic Bibles edited by Felix Pratensis (1516–1517) and Jacob ben Chayyim (1524–1525).[8]

One common and oft-repeated misconception involves a decision purportedly made by a group of Jewish scholars at a conference held in Jamnia (Yavne), a major ancient city on the southern coastal plain of Israel, in A.D. 90. Old Testament scholar Walter C. Kaiser Jr. notes three flaws in the notion that this meeting determined which books would be part of the Jewish canon. First, the deliberations of the council were not binding on any person or group. Second, as far as is known, only two books were discussed—Ecclesiastes and the Song of Solomon—and the discussions about these books involved their interpretation, not their canonicity. Third, the books treated as canonical did not differ from the first-century list found in the writings of Josephus.[9]

In contrast to a decision by committee, we believe the Old Testament canon evolved out of a progressive recognition that certain books were divinely authoritative and canonical from the time of their writing. These books were deemed canonical by contemporaries of the authors, and thus by people who were in the best position to determine whether the claims of the biblical authors were accurate and true. Some books were immediately accepted, others rejected, and still others considered questionable. This view is different from one that contends that canonicity was bestowed at some point long after the writing of the books, at a time when they had already been venerated for decades and centuries.[10]

In Roman Catholicism and Eastern Orthodoxy, seven books beyond the thirty-nine accepted by Protestants and Jews are considered deuterocanonical—that is, canonical but with a secondary status. These books are Tobit, Judith, Wisdom of Solomon, Ecclesiasticus (also called Sira, the Wisdom of Jesus Ben Sirach, or similar titles), Baruch, and 1 and 2 Maccabees. Beyond these, Eastern Orthodoxy also accepts Psalm 151 and 3 and 4 Maccabees. The Roman Catholic books were given canonical status at the Council of Trent in 1546.[11]

We sum up this section with these words by Walter C. Kaiser Jr.:

> There is no evidence that any group, council, or any other religious or nonreligious body made such a decision, much less left a clue as to what their criteria were. Rather, the writers themselves evidenced an unusual awareness that what they were writing was not only a divine revelation from God, but also that it was part and parcel of an ongoing body of communications from God. The accuracy of

such bold claims was scrutinized by their contemporaries, who were in a much better position to assess these claims than subsequent generations. They judged them to be different and separate from other writings or words those same authors expressed on other occasions or even by other authors. Herein lies the essence of the argument for the canon of the Old Testament.[12]

31. When was the canonization of the New Testament completed?

The canon of the New Testament was complete by the end of the first century A.D. in the sense that, by that time, all of the twenty-seven New Testament books had been written, the final one being Revelation by the apostle John. However, because Christianity was expanding numerically and geographically, it took time for all Christians to have knowledge of and access to all of the New Testament writings. By the middle of the second century, many of the books we now have in the New Testament had been collected into some form of a canon.

The words of Jesus and the apostles were important to the early Christians, and guarding their accuracy was part of the church's growth process. Likewise, the history of early Christianity as recorded in the book of Acts was important to maintain. Christianity was born with part of its Bible already present and accessible: the Jewish Scriptures, which Christians came to call the Old Testament. To these books were then added the Greek Scriptures or New Testament. Both were understood to be God's authoritative revelation, as demonstrated in 1 Timothy 5:18, where the Old Testament and the words of Jesus are given equal weight: "For the Scripture says, 'YOU SHALL NOT MUZZLE THE OX WHILE HE IS THRESHING [Deut. 25:4],' and 'The laborer is worthy of his wages [Luke 10:7].'"

The new Christian books were read and used in public worship, becoming a central part of the gathering of Christians. The books of the New Testament were written in order to record the eyewitness accounts of the life and ministry of Jesus, the work of the apostles, and to provide guidance and doctrine for Christians. The guidance and doctrine was for the spiritual growth of Christians as well as for the combating of false prophets, false teaching, and heresy.

Early in the history of Christianity, books of the New Testament were widely known and referenced. For example, the early church father Clement of Rome (ca. 60–100) mentions at least seven books; Ignatius of Antioch (ca. 60–117) speaks of or alludes to ten; Polycarp (ca. 69–155), who was a disciple of John, mentions sixteen; and Justin Martyr (ca. 100–165) knew of at least thirteen. Marcion (ca. 140), although a heretic who rejected the Old Testament, nevertheless accepted eleven New Testament books. Irenaeus (ca. 130–202) writes of twenty-four distinct books, and Hippolytus (ca. 170–235) mentions twenty-five. These and other fathers such as Clement of Alexandria, Tertullian, Origen, Eusebius of Caesarea, and Athanasius show wide knowledge of New Testament writings as well as a progressive recognition of the canon.[13]

While the majority of the books of the New Testament were recognized as canonical by the early or middle of the second century, several books, such as Hebrews, James, 2 Peter, 2 and 3 John, and Jude, were shrouded with uncertainty and disagreement. There were several reasons for this. The apostolic authorship of Hebrews was questioned in the West. It was uncertain which James wrote the book of James, and the book seemed to lack a doctrinal distinctive. Apparent differences in style and vocabulary between 1 Peter and 2 Peter put the latter book under scrutiny. The letters of 2 and 3 John were questioned because of their personal nature and brevity. In verse 17 of Jude, the author seems to set himself apart from the other apostles, and therefore the apostolic standing of the writer was questioned.[14] However, these issues were gradually resolved, and the books were fully recognized as part of the New Testament canon.

As Christianity spread, differences emerged between the canons of the Western and Eastern churches. The Eastern church included in its canon books that were considered helpful for reading in church, though they were not considered divinely inspired Scripture. As already noted, by the early second century, twenty-one New Testament books were generally accepted without dispute in the West; however, in the East, that number was slightly higher and included a larger number of disputed or uncertain books. The different lists in the East continued into the fifth century, until by the end of that century there was agreement within the Eastern church.[15]

As different synods and councils met in the first few centuries to address various doctrinal issues and practices, Eastern and Western Christians interacted regarding canonicity. Among those synods and councils, the Synod of Laodicea in A.D. 363 declared that only the Old Testament, including the Apocrypha, and the twenty-seven books we now have in the New Testament were to be read in the churches. The Council of Hippo (393) affirmed the same twenty-seven books. The Synod of Carthage (397) listed the Old and New Testament books it believed to be canonical and declared that only canonical books should be viewed as authoritative and read in the churches. The Council of Carthage (419) reaffirmed the canon of Scripture and stated that the book of Hebrews should be listed with the other letters of Paul.[16]

One of the most significant documents of early Christianity dealing with the Canon is a document known as the Muratorian Fragment or Muratorian Canon. It is the oldest known list of New Testament books (the next oldest being the list in Eusebius, *Ecclesiastical History* 3.25). Discovered in 1740 by Ludovico Antonio Muratori in Milan, this document is an eighth-century Latin manuscript that contains an early list of New Testament books, citing twenty-two of the twenty-seven. The list does not contain Hebrews, James, 1 and 2 Peter, and 3 John. (It also includes two books not in the New Testament: the Apocalypse of Peter and the Wisdom of Solomon.) The eighty-five-line manuscript contains internal cues suggesting that it is a translation of a much earlier list drawn up in Rome and written about A.D. 170 or 190 (and no later than the fourth century). The document, incomplete and mutilated at the first, begins with Luke but may have originally also listed Matthew and Mark, because it says that Luke is the third gospel.

In addition to the books listed in it, the Muratorian Fragment sheds light on principles by which the New Testament canon was determined. In brief, the following questions were asked concerning each of the books:

- Was the book written either by an apostle or someone with recognized authority in the earliest years of Christianity?
- Does the book agree with the canon of truth—that is, does it reflect apostolic teaching?
- Does the book have wide and early acceptance by Christians in both Eastern and Western churches?
- Does the book have a self-authenticating divine nature?

More on these principles is discussed in the question, "What criteria were used to include or exclude a book from the Bible?"

It is important to remember the difference between the determination of the canon versus discovery of the canon. Canonicity is determined by God rather than by humans. Books of the Bible are not inspired because individuals or groups of individuals determined them to be canonical. Rather, books are canonical because they are inspired by God, and their God-breathed nature is progressively discovered and understood.

32. What are the pseudepigrapha?

The pseudepigrapha (literally, "false writings") are a collection of sixty-three to sixty-five writings (there is no definitive list), most of which were written over a period of more than 400 years between 250 B.C. and A.D. 200. They were composed after the end of the Old Testament era and throughout the era of Jesus, the New

Testament, and the early church. Originally written by Hellenistic Jewish authors, some of the works may have been expanded or rewritten later by Christians.[17]

Each of the books was written under a pseudonym, usually that of a biblical character such as Abraham, Moses, David, Solomon, Jeremiah, Isaiah, Ezra, and others. The content of the material in the writings and the genres varies widely. Some of the writings are legendary in character, such as Jubilees, the Book of Adam and Eve, and the Martyrdom of Isaiah. Other books purport to be historical, including the Lives of the Prophets and the History of Joseph. Writings such as Ahiqar provide teaching and instruction, while yet others are poetic—Psalms of Solomon and Odes of Solomon, for example. Lastly, some sensational writings are prophetic and apocalyptic in content and style, such as 1 and 2 Enoch, 3 Baruch, Apocalypse of Zephaniah, and the Sibylline Oracles.[18]

Although they are not accepted as part of the Bible and never were seriously considered to be such, they are used in biblical studies for the information they provide regarding the social aspects and thinking of early Judaism during the four centuries in which the books were composed. The pseudepigrapha provide a sense of the popular religious climate and ideas of their age.

Biblical scholar Paul Wegner writes, "Pseudepigraphal books are helpful in showing how doctrines developed in relationship to the New Testament. Several concepts particularly developed and expanded are the Torah, the apocalyptic view of history, the kingdom of God, messianic expectations, the Son of man, this age versus the age to come, and sin and suffering versus righteousness and peace."[19]

It is important to stress that pseudepigraphal books were not formulating biblical doctrine and truth; however, they did represent beliefs that were held and taught—whether rightly or wrongly— before, during, and immediately after the New Testament era.

The works were popular and widely known in the early church. In fact, two references to them appear in the book of Jude. The first is found in verse 9: "But Michael the archangel, when he disputed with the devil and argued about the body of Moses, did not dare pronounce against him a railing judgment, but said, 'The Lord rebuke you!'" Here, Jude is likely citing from the first century pseudepigraphal writing the Assumption of Moses. Deuteronomy 34:1-6 records the death of Moses, but there is no mention made of Satan and Michael struggling over his body. We are simply told that Moses died on Mount Pisgah and his burial place is unknown. While there were many Jewish traditions about the death of Moses, the Bible gives very little information about it. However, during the first century A.D. and the time of Jude, it was written of in the Assumption of Moses. That book is not part of the Bible and is now lost except for a small portion. Although not inspired, parts of it may be valid where the contents do not contradict the Bible or biblical doctrine.

In the verse in question, Jude argues that if Michael, a mighty archangel, showed great respect for another celestial being in deferring his dispute with Satan to the sovereign God, then how much more respect should mere humans show for such beings. The false teachers were wrong in their attitudes as well as their doctrine.

Because Jude was writing under the guidance and inspiration of the Holy Spirit, he was not limited to the contents of the Old Testament for historical information. Details that he and other biblical authors included became part of God's inerrant word once recorded. Biblical authors are not restricted to citing only biblical writings. Even though the latter writings are not inspired, they may contain true statements. Thus, there is no reason to doubt the validity of this conflict between Michael and Satan.[20]

In the second Jude passage, verses 14–15, we read, "It was also about these men that Enoch, in the seventh generation from Adam, prophesied, saying, "Behold, the Lord came with many thousands of His holy ones, to execute judgment upon all, and to convict all the ungodly of all their ungodly deeds which they have done in an ungodly way, and of all the harsh things which ungodly sinners have spoken against Him."

Once again, Jude is citing information about a biblical character of whom nothing is found in the Bible other than quick references to Enoch's life and deathless rapture to heaven (Gen. 5:19, 21–24; Heb. 11:5). This time Jude is quoting from the pseudepigraphal Book of Enoch (1:9), a work written during a 200-year period just before the birth of Jesus.

As in verse 9 of Jude, the non-biblical source for this event does not mean that the occurrence is fabricated or that Jude is mistaken. Just the opposite: because Jude, writing under the inspiration and guidance of the Holy Spirit, recounts Enoch's prophecy as true, we can be certain that it did occur.

Jude is not the only biblical author to cite sources outside the Bible. Paul also did so on several occasions when he quoted from pagan poets (Acts 17:28; 1 Cor. 15:33; Titus 1:12). In so doing, these authors are not implying that the books from which they quote are inspired, but rather, that the truths or events cited are valid. Enoch's prophecy does not give new information to Jude's readers; it was, however, a very early prophecy in biblical history and a good summary of God's coming, universal judgment.[21]

The books of the pseudepigrapha are interesting and helpful in understanding some of the ideas held, rightly and wrongly, during the era of the New Testament; however, they should never be confused with the Bible or the truths of the Bible. Unlike the books of the Apocrypha, the books of the pseudepigrapha did not appear in the Greek or Latin translations of the Bible (Septuagint and Vulgate) and were never considered for inclusion in the Canon.

33. What are the Gnostic Gospels?

The Gnostic Gospels are a group of about fifty-two writings that date from the second to fourth centuries A.D. and claim to have been written by prophets, disciples, apostles, and even Jesus. Although they are commonly called gospels, they are not authoritative and inspired works. They come out of the tradition of Gnosticism, a religious and philosophical view that claimed secret knowledge and wisdom and drew upon imagery from the New Testament, pagan myths, and Platonic and neo-Platonic philosophy. Among the most prominent of the Gnostic Gospels are

- Gospel of Judas (second century)
- Gospel of Mary Magdalene (early to late second century)
- Gospel of Peter (mid-second century)
- Gospel of Thomas (late first to early second century)
- Gospel of Truth (mid-second century)
- Gospel of the Savior (second century)[22]

From this list, the two best-known writings are the Gospel of Thomas and the Gospel of Judas.

The Gospel of Thomas, considered Gnostic by some and called "the fifth gospel" because of its early translation and popularity, contains 114 sayings and proverbs that it claims were made by Jesus.[23] However, unlike the gospels of Matthew, Mark, Luke, and John, there is no sequence or structure to the contents of the writing. Most scholars believe it was written in Syria about A.D. 120–140.

The Gospel of Judas manuscript that is extant is a fourth-century copy of a second-century work (which Irenaeus writes about around A.D. 180 in his work *Against Heresies* 1.31). We know that it was likely written later in the second century because some of the Gnostic terminology that is used in it reflects a developed system of thought (e.g., *aeon* and *luminary*). The work is an attempt to place Jesus' betrayer Judas in a much more favorable light by stating that Judas was Jesus' closest friend and that Jesus told Judas to betray him in order to more quickly accomplish the will of God. Therefore, according to this work, Judas did the right thing by betraying Jesus. However, the Gospel of Judas fails to mention that Judas regretted his betrayal of Jesus and returned the money and committed suicide (Matt. 27:3–5).

Gnosticism was very broad and eclectic and was viewed by the New Testament writers as a pagan false teaching. (Paul's letter to the Colossians, for instance, was in part a defense of Jesus Christ against Gnosticism.) Such writings were never accepted as divinely inspired and canonical, nor were the contents ever considered historically accurate or biblically and doctrinally sound. According to Gnosticism, Jesus did not have a real body but only a spirit which looked to be flesh and bone. (John speaks to this heresy, though not specifically to Gnosticism, in 1 John 4:2–3.) Gnosticism claimed to possess cryptic wisdom, secret knowledge, and mystical experiences.

Until the last few decades, little information was available about Gnosticism apart from what some of the church fathers had written against it (e.g., Irenaeus in *Against Heresies*). In 1945, an ancient library of documents was found in upper Egypt at Nag Hammadi. Among the documents were several Gnostic writings that spoke of Jesus, often in unfamiliar and contradictory ways when compared with the four first-century gospels of the New Testament.

The Gnostic Gospels have received a lot of attention in recent years in popular culture through the writings of Dan Brown, whose 2003 best-selling novel, *The Da Vinci Code*, used them as a background. In scholarly circles, writings by scholars and authors such as Elaine Pagels or Bart Ehrman have argued that the Gnostic writings should cause a reevaluation of the history of Christianity, the Bible, and theology.[24]

Much of the material from the Gnostic writings that was discovered is just now coming to have wide distribution and discussion because of the time involved in gathering and translating the works. As this occurs, there continues to be skepticism and debate about the history of Christianity and the Bible, with the result that the alternative views are receiving popular and scholarly attention. In an interview several years ago, New Testament scholar Darrell Bock articulated insightfully what many have heard of, read, or experienced:

> There's a revolution that's going on in the humanities about how to handle history. The old mantra is that history is

written by the winners. Now we're digging up material by the losers. You read the material by the losers, and then you tweak the history. In some cases you revise it. What I'm trying to do is to explain this movement and then [ask] whether the revision is actually historically valid or not. My premise is that, yes, history is written by the winners. But sometimes, the winners deserved to win.[25]

The Gnostic texts are exciting not because they help us to better understand Christianity—the so-called "alternate Christianity" they propose is no improvement on the genuine article—but because they give us a better understanding of Gnosticism and the environment in which biblical orthodoxy and the Bible flourished. The Gnostic Gospels help us increase our knowledge of the second century, not the first.

34. What is the Apocrypha?

The Apocrypha refers to a group of fourteen or fifteen Jewish writings composed between 200 B.C. and A.D. 100.[26] The difference between fourteen and fifteen books occurs because the Letter of Jeremiah is frequently combined with the book titled Baruch.

The word *apocrypha* is derived from Greek meaning "concealed" or "hidden away." It is used in its plural form (like the word *data*), the singular being *apocryphon*. The Apocrypha is comprised of:

- 1 Esdras
- 2 Esdras
- Tobit
- Judith
- Additions to the Book of Esther
- The Wisdom of Solomon
- Ecclesiasticus (also called the Wisdom of Jesus the Son of Sirach, or sometimes simply Sirach)
- Baruch

- The Letter of Jeremiah
- The Prayer of Azariah and the Song of the Three Young Men
- Susanna
- Bel and the Dragon
- The Prayer of Manasseh
- 1 Maccabees
- 2 Maccabees

There are four genres or categories within the Apocrypha:

- Historical—1 Esdras, 1 Maccabees, 2 Maccabees
- Religious—Tobit, Judith, Susanna, Additions to Esther, Bel and the Dragon
- Wisdom or ethical teaching—Ecclesiasticus (Sirach), Wisdom of Solomon, Baruch (which may include the Letter of Jeremiah), Prayer of Manasseh, Prayer of Azariah
- Apocalyptic—2 Esdras

The books of the Apocrypha were not included in the Hebrew Scriptures, but the Latin Vulgate and the final form of the Greek Old Testament, known as the Septuagint, did include them. Because of the wide use of the Septuagint in the Eastern Church and the dominance of the Latin Vulgate in the Western Church for almost a thousand years, the Apocrypha became well-known, widely used, and rarely questioned as to whether it was truly part of the canon of the Bible. Wegner writes of the early history of the Apocrypha in the East and the West:

> Jews and early Christians drew a distinction between the Hebrew Old Testament and noncanonical material. However, this distinction was not rigidly maintained, so that the two parts of the church dealt with apocryphal books differently. The Eastern Church held to a threefold division of religious books: books that could be read in the

church; books that could be read privately, and books that were not to be read at all. In the Western Church, however, this threefold division was never generally accepted; books were distinguished as either canonical or noncanonical, though the majority of the church fathers in the West still included some apocryphal books in their lists (e.g., Augustine).[27]

The first person to use the word *apocrypha* in reference to the writings was the great biblical scholar and translator of the Vulgate, Jerome (347–420) in *Letter* 107.12.[28] Many Protestants and Jews viewed the Apocrypha as important but not divinely inspired. For Roman Catholics, the books were affirmed as canonical at the Council of Trent during its fourth session in April 1546. For Orthodox Christians, it was the Synod of Jerusalem in 1672 that recognized them as canonical.

Today the Apocryphal books are called "deuterocanonical" by Roman Catholics, based upon a distinction introduced by Dominican theologian Sixtus of Sienna (1520–1569). Sixtus distinguished books in the Septuagint that in his day were considered canonical (he called them "protocanonical") from those that were not. Orthodox Christians use the term *anagignoskomena* for the books of the Apocrypha.

The Protestant Reformers were in agreement the books had value ("bokes proceding from godlie men," according to the Geneva Bible introduction) but rejected them as canonical. Nevertheless, until well after the Protestant Reformation, the Apocrypha was included in many Protestant versions of the Bible, including the Geneva Bible and King James Version (normally placed as a separate section between the Old and New Testaments and printed on smaller type to indicate it was not equal to Scripture). Not until the nineteenth century was the Bible commonly published without the Apocrypha. The omission among English translations of the Bible was tied in part to the printing monopoly in Great Britain, in which only the Crown or its agents (usually Oxford University Press and Cambridge University Press) had the legal right to publish Bibles.

There are numerous arguments that have been advanced for rejecting the Apocrypha as canonical.[29] Among them are the following:

- The New Testament never cites any apocryphal book.
- Jesus' usage of Scripture suggests that only the books of the Hebrew Bible (Old Testament) were considered authoritative (Matt. 23:34–35; Luke 11:50–51).
- The Apocrypha contains significant historical inaccuracies. (E.g., according to Tobit 1:3–5, Tobit lived in Nineveh about 722 B.C., yet he saw the division of the united kingdom in 931 B.C.)
- The Apocrypha never claims to be the Word of God.
- There are theological difficulties. (E.g., prayers for the dead in 2 Maccabees 12:45–46 are contrary to Hebrews 9:27, which teaches that decisions about eternal life must be made before death.)
- Many early church fathers argued against its canonicity (e.g., Melito, Origen, Cyril of Jerusalem, Athanasius, Jerome).
- The pseudonymity of the writings makes them suspect.

Interestingly but perhaps not unexpectedly, images and ideas from the Apocrypha are well represented in art, music, and literature. Paintings of subjects such as Tobit, Judith, and Susanna are part of the heritage of the great masters of European art (e.g., *Tobias and the Angel* by the fifteenth-century Italian artist Andrea del Verrocchio). The Apocrypha is found in the works of Chaucer, Shakespeare, Milton, Longfellow, and others. In hymnody, there are ideas and phrases from it in "Now Thank We All Our God" (dependent on Martin Luther's translation of Sirach 50:22–24 and written by Martin Rinkart about 1636, when the devastating Thirty Years War was nearing its end), "O Come, O Come, Emmanuel," "It Came Upon a Midnight Clear," and many of the hymns of Charles

Wesley.[30] It has often been said that Christopher Columbus used 2 Esdras 6:42, which states that the ratio of land to water is six to one, to convince Queen Isabella and King Ferdinand of Spain to fund his search for a new route to India. Examples such as these show the enormous influence of the Bible and religious literature on Western culture and values. Though not canonical, the Apocrypha has had an important religious, cultural, and literary history.

PART 6

The Composition of the Bible

35. What was the physical process of writing the Bible?

The revelation of God in written form has been recorded on a variety of surfaces. The Ten Commandments were inscribed on the side of a rock in the Sinai. Some of the sources which Moses may have used in developing the family histories in the Pentateuch were probably written on baked clay similar to what was used by the Hittites, Assyrians, and Babylonians. As far as is known, however, almost none of the sacred texts were recorded on similar material, one of the exceptions being the Aaronic blessing on a silver amulet found in Jerusalem by archaeologist Gabriel Barkay.[1]

Papyrus was plenteous in Egypt, created from the papyrus reeds in the Nile, and it is likely that this was used by Moses in composing the books of the Old Testament that bear his name. Papyrus scrolls are made by cutting papyrus reeds into strips, squeezing the water from them, and placing them crisscross until a large sheet is created. Then the finished product is put under considerable pressure until the fabric becomes uniform in consistency. The resulting material is very strong, and in an arid area such as Egypt it could last for hundreds of years. Papyri scrolls have been known to last from more than two hundred years, even in non-desert climates.

Some of the Old Testament may have been copied onto animal skins; however, the better fabric, and one that replaced papyri, was parchment, also known as vellum. It was a refined animal skin and very durable. Whereas the earlier books of the New Testament were written on papyrus leaves, the later codices such as the fourth- and fifth-century Sinaiticus, Vaticanus, and Alexandrinus were written on parchment and are still extant in readable form. Pergamum, a location of one of the seven churches in Asia Minor (modern Turkey), became a major producer and exporter of parchment and thus grew very wealthy.

Carved sticks and reeds were the common pens of the ancient world. They were dipped in a thick, dark ink made of elements such as soot mixed with gum or alum. Since the writing surfaces for ink were precious and expensive, it was common for individuals to first write out their words on hardened, smooth wax tablets. The words would then be copied onto the papyrus or vellum, after which the tablets were restored for reuse by means of a heated metal instrument that smoothed the wax.

The Old and New Testament documents were mostly written with the help of scribes, who would transcribe the words spoken by the prophet or apostle. We know, based on practices of the Graeco-Roman world, that more than one copy of any given New Testament manuscript was probably made. The author would keep one copy and send one or more of the others to their recipients.

36. How did the authors use their sources in writing the Bible?

The authors of the Old and New Testaments composed their works in a number of ways. Sometimes, as with Moses, they set forth the words of God with the expectation that the works would stay in existence. The Torah, for instance, was not only read to the people, but a copy was also placed in the Ark of the Covenant.

Much of the information that is found in the first five books of the Bible after Genesis was based on Moses' own personal experience.

Genesis 38 and following seems to come from oral tradition that was passed down through the Hebrew people about the man Joseph. Genesis 1 through 37 would be based on both oral tradition and maybe some clay documents. Certainly the family histories mentioned throughout the book, including the genealogies, were probably records that were kept and then used by Moses in writing Genesis.

What about the creation account? Obviously no human was present, so God had to reveal the events of creation to Adam and Eve or their immediate descendants, who in turn passed the information down from one generation to the next. It is also possible that Moses received the creation narrative by a vision or other revelatory means. Those who wrote the Chronicles may have drawn on a variety of sources, since their writings refer to extra-canonical works, and since their work closely resembles the books of 1 and 2 Kings.

In the New Testament, the apostle who relies most heavily on the Old Testament for writing his book was John, while on the island of Patmos. The Gospels were written to present different, but not contradictory, views of Jesus. The Epistles, on the other hand, were written to respond to problems within the churches. This is especially true of 1 Corinthians, in which Paul responds to personal information that he received from members of the Corinthian church, and to a letter from the church which he seems to address point by point in the latter half of the book.

37. How were scribes used in producing the books of the Bible?

Probably most of the books in the Old Testament were transcribed by scribes such as Baruch, Jeremiah's assistant who recorded his master's visions.

The authors of the New Testament also probably used scribes in most instances. We know specifically of Silas, Silvanus, and Mark. The gospel authors were either eyewitnesses or received their information from those who were eyewitnesses. Matthew and John, in the authors' understanding, were disciples of Christ, with John having access to special revelations from Christ, similar to James and Peter. Mark seems to have been Peter's scribe, recording his recollections; and Luke carefully researched a number of sources for his gospel in order to present an accurate account.

38. Did the authors write in different styles?

The various styles found in the biblical text are not as obvious in the English translations as in the Hebrew, Aramaic, and Greek texts, where the differences often are pronounced. In contemporary English translations, one may see that a number of Old Testament books, and even some New Testament books, include poetic style, particularly in the Psalms and Prophets. Moreover, Paul quotes hymns, such as Philippians 2:5–12 and 1 Timothy 3:16, and John in the Revelation uses a variety of literary forms. Much of this can be seen in translation.

Not so readily apparent are the levels of original-language syntactical and grammatical forms, the untranslatable clues that reflect a more polished command of Greek, and the varied depths of vocabulary. For example, John's theology is profound but his Greek is simple, whereas Paul uses good Greek with great intensity. He also writes lengthy sentences joined together by many conjunctions and dependent clauses. Mark's gospel is crisp, fast-moving, simple Greek. Hebrews, on the other hand, is among the finest examples of high-level Greek, reminiscent of the classical period of Athens—as should be expected of its writer, a person influenced by the neo-classical renaissance at Alexandria Egypt. In contrast, 2 Peter appears rougher and in our view may have been written by Peter without the help of Silvanus, who served as the apostle's scribe in writing 1 Peter.

PART 7

The Transcription and Transmission of the Bible

39. Why didn't God preserve the original text?

This question is difficult to answer. Our first inclination is to say, we don't know. But we can speculate. A plausible explanation is this: Although God could have preserved the actual manuscripts authored by Moses, Isaiah, David, Matthew, Paul, and the like, He has generally let the laws of nature operate as He established them. He rarely alters a storm, though storms often bring devastation. He allows us to die, due to our guilt incurred through the sin of Adam, even though the sufferings of His people grieve Him. And He has allowed the original Hebrew, Aramaic, and Greek manuscripts to decay; yet He has also preserved His Word through the careful copying of many manuscripts in which we have great reason to trust, confident that they contain the words of God.

We must remember that the Hebrew text which Jesus called Scripture had already gone through the same process as the New Testament underwent later on, yet Jesus had confidence in the Torah that He read and quoted. It was not a word-for-word rendering of the actual Hebrew manuscripts that preceded the time of Christ, but nothing is lacking in the theology of the Old Testament that Jesus taught. As Jesus trusted the Scriptures of His time, so we too can have confidence in our current Hebrew and Greek texts. We have reasonable assurance that no doctrine of Scripture is impacted by any minor problems with the documents that have been passed down to us.

40. What is textual criticism?

Textual criticism is the study of manuscripts (or printings, in the case of books written after the advent of the printing press) to determine the original form of a text. It is the method of determining what was said in the original manuscripts of the Bible. It can be used with any piece of literature and is not limited to the study of the biblical text. With respect to the Bible, textual criticism is a discipline used to recover the original wording of the Bible. Because the original manuscripts of the Bible no longer exist, it is necessary to compare and study the thousands of copies of the original manuscripts to determine the reading of the original text. Textual criticism is the study used to answer the question, "Do we have now what they had then?" It is the process of making sense of the textual variants of the thousands of biblical manuscripts.

Not all manuscripts have the same words, phrases, or passages. Sometimes things are added or omitted, and as a result, English translations that are used today contain some variations in verses. Examples of this are found in Matthew 6:13, 25; Mark 3:14; 9:29; 16:8; Luke 8:43; John 3:13; 7:53–8:11; Acts 8:36; Ephesians 1:1; Colossians 1:14; and 1 John 5:7–8.[1] Perhaps the most well-known discrepancy involves the last twelve verses of Mark (16:9–20), which do not appear in two of the most trustworthy manuscripts of the New Testament.[2]

Variations in the manuscripts fall into two categories: unintentional and intentional. Ninety-five percent are the former kind. They are natural mistakes made by copyists when copying from one manuscript to another—much like a typographical error one makes when typing on a keyboard. Unintentional errors include the following:

- Errors of sight
- Confusion of letters that are similar in appearance

- Faulty division of words in a sentence
- Omission of letters, words, or sentences
- Skipping words because of copying words or sentences that end with similar words
- Mistakenly repeating words or sentences
- Mistakenly changing the order of letters or words
- Errors of hearing
- Errors of writing[3]

Intentional errors can involve any of these:

- Revisions of grammar and spelling
- Harmonization of similar passages
- Elimination of apparent discrepancies and difficulties
- Conflations of the text
- Adapting of different liturgical traditions
- Making theological or doctrinal changes[4]

The potential for each of these human errors is quite understandable for anyone who has ever typed or copied a document. But it is important to realize that the amount of material under study in such cases is a small percentage of the biblical text (although there are a lot of textual variants).[5] Moreover, no Christian doctrine rests on the words and verses that are disputed. Textual critic Daniel Wallace concludes, "Suffice it to say that viable textual variants that disturb cardinal doctrines found in the NT have not yet been produced."[6]

When textual variants are studied, the criteria used to evaluate them are divided into two groups: external evidence and internal evidence. External evidence includes as the following details:

- The date or age of the manuscript witness
- The type of text embodied in the manuscript (based on one of several textual traditions that were geographically grouped, such as Western text, Byzantine text, Syriac text,

Caesarean text, and Alexandrian text; see accompanying map of textual traditions that shows where these traditions were located)

- The geographical distribution of the textual witnesses
- The genealogical relationship of the texts

The Geographical Centers of New Testament Text Types[7]

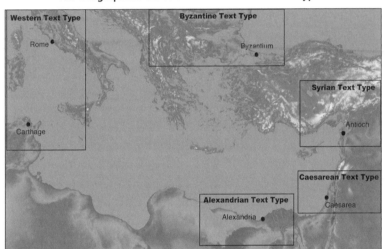

Assessing manuscripts by their internal evidence requires knowledge of ancient writing and scribal habits. It also involves the ability to evaluate what the original authors were most likely to have written, using a variety of criteria as follows:

- The more awkward or grammatically unusual a text, the likelier it is to be the original because of the tendency of scribes to make a text read more smoothly.
- The shortest reading of a text is probably the original, because scribes tended to add additional information or phrases from parallel passages for clarity.
- The older of texts is given more weight because of its historical proximity to the original text (everything else being equal).

- Manuscripts that are geographically diverse are usually the ones with the original readings.
- Explaining how variants could have occurred is extremely important.
- The analysis of a given biblical author's literary style, vocabulary, and theology in the same book is used to decide probable original wording.
- The texts that are doctrinally weaker, especially those relating to major theological discussions during the period of manuscript changes, *may* be preferred when balanced with all other criteria.[8]

How might all of this work? An example might be variations on a text where some manuscripts read, "Lord Jesus," and others read, "Lord Jesus Christ." The textual critic then decides to determine which was written in the original text. Both phrases are used in the New Testament; however, if there was a question about the reading, one could logically expect the transcriptionist to have chosen the first version in order to harmonize it with other texts, and also because it is the shorter reading. This simple illustration is not always the textual answer, but it shows how a variant might be approached.

New Testament scholar Arthur G. Patzia explains the importance of textual criticism for us: "The work of textual criticism is never complete or precise because more manuscripts are being discovered, translated, and evaluated."[9] Rather than eroding trust in the reliability of the Bible, textual criticism is something that should increase our trust in the Bible we hold in our hands.

41. What are the oldest copies of the Bible in existence?

The oldest copies of the Hebrew text that we possess are those that were found in approximately 1948 in the Dead Sea area at a place known as Qumran. Essene scribes had carefully and methodically copied the Hebrew text for nearly two centuries before the Essenes fell under the Romans in A.D. 70. The earliest

Hebrew manuscripts that we had prior to the Dead Sea Scrolls, done by the Masoretes, dated to A.D. 900; but with finding the Dead Sea Scrolls, our manuscript evidence traced back a thousand years earlier. What is fascinating is how very closely these two groups of manuscripts agree.

The Greek New Testament manuscripts number in excess of 5,700, with another nearly 10,000 translations into Latin, Syriac, Coptic, and other ancient languages. The earliest copies of portions of the New Testament date within 100 years of the events recorded in them—a marked contrast with the many centuries between copies and events found in other writings of the Graeco-Roman world. For example, a portion of a copy of John 18 exists from the early part of the second century (between 100–150, the latter date being most likely), while the original work was written in Ephesus between 85–90. Many other incomplete but substantial portions of the New Testament are extant toward the end of the second century and the beginning of the third. By the early fourth century, entire copies of the New Testament are available.

In contrast to all other sources of the ancient world, the Old and New Testaments have wonderfully attested and accurate manuscript copies, with only a small portion of significant differences existing among them.

Old Testament Manuscripts[10]			
Name	**Original Date of Composition***	**Date of Earliest Copy**	**Books**
Dead Sea Scrolls	15th or 13th to 4th century B.C.	250 B.C.–A.D. 68	Includes 223-plus biblical manuscripts from every book of the Hebrew Bible except Esther
Dead Sea Isaiah Scroll (1QIsaa)	8th century B.C.	150–100 B.C.	Only complete Hebrew copy of the entire book of Isaiah

continued . . .

Old Testament Manuscripts *continued*			
Name	**Original Date of Composition***	**Date of Earliest Copy**	**Books**
Dead Sea Scroll 1 Samuel (4QSam-b)	10th to 9th century B.C.	4th to 3rd century B.C.	Contains 1 Samuel 16, 19, 21, 23; perhaps the oldest Dead Sea manuscript to date
Rylands Papyrus 485	15th or 13th century B.C.	150 B.C.	Contains Greek portions of Deuteronomy 23–28
Nash Papyrus	15th or 13th century B.C.	150 B.C.–A.D. 68	Damaged portion of the Decalogue. Exodus 20; Deuteronomy 5:6–21; Shema 6:4–9
Peshitta	15th or 13th to 4th century B.C.	A.D. 100–200	Entire Old Testament in Syriac
Chester Beatty Papyri	15th or 13th to 8th century B.C.	A.D. 150	Contains large portions of Genesis, Numbers, Deuteronomy, Isaiah, Jeremiah, Daniel, Esther, and Ecclesiastes
Targum of Onkelos	15th or 13th century B.C.	A.D. 200	Torah
Codex Vaticanus (B)	15th or 13th to 4th century B.C.	A.D. 325	The Old Testament and Apocrypha in Greek uncial except portions of Genesis, 2 Kings, Psalms, 1 and 2 Maccabees, and the Prayer of Manesses
Codex Ephraemi Rescriptus	13th to 10th centuries B.C.	A.D. 345	Contains Job, Proverbs, Ecclesiastes, Song of Solomon
Codex Sinaiticus (א)	13th to 4th centuries B.C.	A.D. 350	Half of the Old Testament in Greek uncial
Latin Vulgate	A.D. 390–405		Entire Old Testament in Latin
Codex Alexandrinus (A)	13th to 4th centuries B.C.	A.D. 450	Entire Old Testament in Greek uncial

British Museum Oriental 4445	13th century B.C.	A.D. 850	Pentateuch
Codex Cairensis (C)	13th to 4th centuries B.C.	A.D. 895	Former and latter prophets
Aleppo Codex	13th to 4th centuries B.C.	A.D. 900	Oldest complete Hebrew text of the Old Testament
Leningrad Codex	8th to 4th centuries B.C.	A.D. 916	Isaiah, Jeremiah, Ezekiel
Codex Leningradensis B-19A (L)	13th to 4th centuries B.C.	A.D. 1008	Complete Hebrew text of the Old Testament
Samaritan Pentateuch (SP)	13th century B.C.	10th to 11th centuries A.D.	Pentateuch written in Samaritan characters

*Whether the books of Moses were composed in the 15th century B.C. or the 13th century B.C. depends on how one views the date of the exodus, as late as 15th century or early 13th century B.C. Most conservative scholars embrace the earlier date, thus around 1440 B.C. for composition of the Pentateuch, while some conservative scholars and most liberal scholars prefer the early 13th century B.C. for its composition.

New Testament Manuscripts[11]				
Name	Books	Original Date of Autograph	Earliest Date of Copy	Gap from Original
John Rylands Fragment (P52)	Selection of the gospel of John, includes John 18:31–33, 37–38 and is considered the oldest New Testament fragment known	A.D. 85–100	A.D. 125	25–40 years
Chester Beatty Papyri (P45, 46, 47)	Contains portions of Matthew, Mark, Luke, John, Pauline epistles, and the book of Revelation	A.D. 50–100	A.D. 200–300	100–250 years
Bodmer Papyri (P66, 72, 75)	Substantial portions of the gospel of John and the earliest copy of 1 and 2 Peter and Jude	A.D. 50–70	A.D. 175–200	105–150 years

continued . . .

New Testament Manuscripts *continued*				
Name	**Books**	**Original Date of Autograph**	**Earliest Date of Copy**	**Gap from Original**
Codex Vaticanus (B)	Contains most of the Greek Old Testament and the majority of the New Testament	A.D. 50–100	A.D. 325	225–275 years
Codex Sinaiticus (א)	Earliest copy of a complete New Testament except for several verses: Mark 16 and John 7 and 8; also includes over half the Greek Old Testament (Septuagint, LXX)	A.D. 50–100	A.D. 350	250–300 years
Codex Alexandrinus (A)	Written in uncial Greek script, Alexandrinus possesses the entire Old Testament and most of the new	A.D. 50–100	5th century A.D.	350–400 years
Codex Ephraemi (C)	Ephraemi was erased in the 12th century and then restored by Constantine Tischendorf in the 19th century. It contains portions of every book in the New Testament except 2 Thessalonians and 2 John	A.D. 50–100	A.D. 450	350–400 years
Codex Bezae (D)	The manuscript is a rare Greek and Latin bilingual text of portions of the Gospels, Acts, and 3 John 11–15; 3 John is in Latin only	A.D. 50–65	5th–6th centuries A.D.	400–500 years

Magdalen Papyrus	Small fragment of Matthew 26:7–8, 10, 14–15. German scholar Carsten Thiede argued for middle to late 1st century. If he's correct, the fragment would be the oldest manuscript of the New Testament.	A.D. 40–65	A.D. 75–200	10–160 years
Codex Clara-montanus (D2)	Bilingual Greek/Latin manuscript of the Pauline Epistles, including Hebrews	A.D. 50–64	6th century A.D.	500 years
Codex Washing-tonianus	Contains the four gospels	A.D. 50–100	4th–5th centuries A.D.	250–400 years

42. How close to the original manuscripts are those manuscripts used for our translations?

Do our translations reflect the best reading of the original or early copies of the originals? That depends largely on the manuscripts used by translators. Most textual criticism scholars agree that New Testament manuscripts dating from the fifth century A.D. and before will provide a better reading than Byzantine manuscripts of the tenth century and afterward. And Old Testament manuscripts, which were copied even more carefully than the New Testament, represent a reliable basis for the translation of the Bible. No major teaching of Scripture is in any danger of distortion or omission due to insufficient source documents.

43. What happened to the original manuscripts, and how long did the autographs remain in existence?

No one knows what happened to the original manuscripts of Scripture, and the difficult problem is that if we actually had the originals, we would not know them from early copies of the original. There is some evidence that some of the original New Testament manuscripts existed into the late second century A.D.,[12] but since they were on papyrus and in wet climates rather than the desert, they probably perished within a couple of hundred years of their writing. Fortunately, copies of these originals were made during this time, so that what we have is far more accurate than mere copies of copies of copies. Rather, we have early copies that were checked directly against the original texts by the copyists, and subsequently, good copies checked against those early copies.

PART 8

The Translation of the Bible

44. What is the Masoretic Text?

The Masoretic Text (MT) is the Old Testament Hebrew text that we know today and the text from which all English translations of the Old Testament are derived. Accepted as the authorized text, "it is the starting point for textual critics in their attempts to reconstruct the original text, and the standard text to which all other ancient Hebrew manuscripts (such as the biblical manuscripts of the Dead Sea Scrolls) are compared."[1] The Masoretic Text is derived from a group of texts preserved by Jewish scribes and scholars known as the Masoretes during the sixth through eleventh centuries.

The amazing history of the Bible includes the copying, collating, and passing down of its text through the centuries. Anyone who has seen or practiced calligraphy will appreciate the care and skill required to copy a text. Such an appreciation gives a glimpse into the world of preserving and duplicating the biblical text. For example, during the time from 100 B.C. to A.D. 400, Jewish scribes who copied biblical texts and commentary on them developed detailed rules for copying and making notations about words in the texts.

This not only standardized the necessary process of copying the texts by hand, but it also provided many details about the text.

By the sixth century A.D., the Hebrew text and the careful annotations of it were passed to a new generation of scribes known as the Masoretes. These scribes inherited detailed protocols and procedures for carefully maintaining the Old Testament texts and the scrolls on which they were written. They upheld these practices and made meticulous notes about the biblical text and scrolls, which included such painstaking details as the number of letters used in a biblical book. The Masoretes even counted to determine the middle letter in a book. Everything that could possibly be counted in a book was counted and recorded.

The Hebrew alphabet doesn't have vowels. It is all consonants. So the Masoretes added vowel points and accents to the texts during this time.[2] This made reading easier for those unfamiliar with a text, and it eliminated confusion over words. For example, does "rd stp" mean "red step" or "road stop"? Normally, this was clear from context and other texts, but sometimes confusion arose. The vowel points clarified such difficulties. The Masoretes also added accents to the text to facilitate correct pronunciation.

The Masorah was also added and used in the margins of the scrolls and codices. The Masorah is a collection of notations about the text, including such things as alternate readings and different grammatical forms. It was intended to preserve the accuracy of the Hebrew text. Because of their high view of the text, the scribes did not want to alter the text, so they instituted this system of marginal notes and marks to clarify textual questions.

Two schools of scribes were involved in producing the Masoretic Text: an Eastern (Babylonian) and Western (Palestinian) school. The Western school was further separated into two branches of scribal families. Around the year A.D. 925, the first complete Hebrew Bible was produced by a Jewish scribe named Aaron ben Asher (d. ca. 960), the head of one of the two Western-branch families of scribes. This very important text is known as the Aleppo

Codex, because for centuries the work was kept in the Jewish community of Aleppo, Syria.[3] Today, the Aleppo Codex is located at Hebrew University in Jerusalem.

Among the most important of the surviving manuscripts of the Masoretic tradition are:

- Codex Cairensis (A.D. 895)
- Aleppo Codex (ca. A.D. 930)
- Oriental 4445 (ca. A.D. 950 and ca. 1540)
- Codex Leningradensis (ca. A.D. 1008)
- Petersburg Codex of the Prophets (A.D. 916)
- Codex Reuchlinianus of the Prophets (A.D. 1105)
- Erfurtensis Codex (A.D. 1000–1300)[4]

The work of the Masoretes in accurately transcribing and preserving medieval biblical texts was a remarkable achievement. For more than a thousand years since their work (as well as before), there has been a reliable witness to the original text of the Old Testament.

45. What are the different translation theories?

Anyone who has taken a foreign language class in school or set out to learn another language knows that accurately conveying ideas from one language to another is not easy. Regardless of whether the endeavor is spoken or written, the work of translation is difficult. It becomes even more so when working across cultures and history.

As far as the mechanics of translation are concerned, it doesn't matter if one is translating the *Bhagavad Gita* (Sanskrit), *Beowulf* (Old English), or the Bible (Hebrew, Aramaic, and Greek). Nor does it matter what language is the receptor language (in our case, English). However, as Christians, we believe that unlike other books, the Bible is the divinely inspired, infallible, and inerrant Word of God. It is God's words that are being translated, guided, and written through the individual styles of human agents; it is not the words of fallible human authors who are merely recording their own musings, opinions, or ideas. Therefore, care should be taken to translate the material in such a way that it remains a translation rather than an interpretation or a paraphrase.

Translators today are guided by two major translation theories: *formal equivalence* and *dynamic equivalence*. Each theory has strong proponents and English Bible versions derived from it. The many Bible versions available today can be placed on a spectrum within these two categories (unless they are paraphrased editions of the Bible rather than translations, in which case they are in a third category).

Formal equivalence is the theory and practice that was used in Bible translation until the middle of the twentieth century. Formal equivalence is basically word-for-word translation, or what is known today in Bible translation as *essentially literal* translation. Using this theory in English Bible translation, translators assumed that the goal of translating the Bible into English is to "translate the words of the original Hebrew and Greek texts insofar as the process of translations allows [us] . . . to reproduce into English the words of the original."[5] Adherents of this model attempt to provide an English equivalent for every word, highlighting where words are added to make the translation more understandable and following the original word order where possible.[6]

Dynamic equivalence is not a word-for-word translation endeavor, but a thought-for-thought translation that is frequently termed *functional equivalence*. Proponents of dynamic equivalence aim to reproduce the ideas or thoughts of the original text rather than its words. "Dynamic equivalence is a theory of translation based on the premise that whenever something in the original text is foreign or unclear to a contemporary English reader, the original text should be translated in terms of an equivalent rather than literally."[7]

The concern that has been expressed over dynamic equivalence (and with which we agree) is that it takes undue liberties in translation that ultimately destabilize the biblical text. English scholar

Leland Ryken observes that "once we adopt the premise that it is only the thought of the Bible that needs to be translated, and not the words, then once a translation committee decides what a passage means, it is free to use whatever English words it wishes to express what it thinks the meaning of the passage is."[8] Often, part of this process involves reducing the level of the vocabulary of the original text, dropping figurative language, changing gender references, and shortening sentences.[9] The result, in part, is also a plethora of translations of varying degrees of reliability and accuracy.

Why does all this matter? It affects the version of the Bible that one chooses to use. That, in part, is why so many English translations and versions of the Bible are available: each one is based upon a translation theory. We should therefore carefully consider the Bible version we choose to use and understand what it is. Every version has an introduction that presents the guiding principles for its translation.[10]

46. How close to the meaning of the original Hebrew and Greek are our translations?

Theories of translation are a major problem in translation work today. Since the days of linguist Eugene Nida, who was instrumental in taking the Bible to new language groups, the theory of dynamic translation has been popular. This was never so until recent days. Reaching from all the way back to the Greek and Latin translations of the first century A.D. to most English translations before the middle of the last century, formal equivalence was the guiding translational theory. Dynamic equivalence is more concerned with conveying the meaning of a given biblical text in simple language, whereas formal equivalence is more concerned with bringing over the very words of Scripture, to the greatest extent possible, leaving the meaning of the passage more in the hands of the reader.[11]

Published in its entirety in 1560, the Geneva Bible served as a foundation for the masterful King James Version (1611). Listen to the words of its translators in the preface:

Now as we have chiefly observed the sense, and labored always to restore it to all integrity, so have we most reverently kept the propriety of the words, considering that the Apostles who spake and wrote to the Gentiles in the Greek tongue, rather constrained them to the lively phrase of the Hebrew than enterprised far by mollifying their language to speak as the Gentiles did. And for this and other causes we have in many places reserved the Hebrew phrases, notwithstanding that they may seem somewhat hard in their ears that are not well practiced and also delight in the sweet-sounding phrases of the Holy Scriptures.

47. Why are there so many English versions and translations?

The Bible remains the best-selling book in the world. The variety of English translations and versions is due in part to the different translation theories that are the foundation for each version, and in part to the commercial market that not only publishes Bibles for reading, worship, and study, but also directs their publications toward niche markets (e.g., students, age groups, occupations, interests).

Not all English Bibles are of equal quality or reliability. In determining which translation to use for a primary Bible, there are several principles to consider:[12]

- Accuracy—use a Bible that is accurate.
- Fidelity—use a Bible that is faithful to the original words.
- Clarity—use a Bible that uses clarity of diction and expression of words and ideas.
- Orthodoxy—use a Bible that allows theology to be derived from the text rather than one where the text is derived from theology.
- Transparency—use a Bible that opens the world of the Bible to you.
- Poetry—use a Bible that is faithful to the literary forms and

genres of the text, such as the one-third of the Bible that is poetic and uses such devices as imagery, allusion, figure of speech, and metaphor.

- Dignity and beauty—use a Bible that provides an elevating experience for you as the reader at all levels: aesthetic, intellectual, emotional, and theological.

Considering these principles and others requires an investment of time in researching, sampling, and comparing Bible versions before selecting a Bible for regular use. But doing so will reward the reader enormously. When Jesus read the Scriptures, He did so carefully and thoughtfully. So should we.

48. What is the Septuagint?

The Septuagint, from the Latin word *septuaginta* for "seventy," is also abbreviated as LXX due to a legend that it was compiled in seventy days by seventy scholars. It is a Greek translation of the Old Testament that was produced between 250–100 B.C. It was the first translation of the Hebrew Bible (or any book of that size in the ancient world).[13]

The Septuagint was used extensively by the authors of the New Testament books as well as by non-Christian writers of the era such as Flavius Josephus and Philo. Many of the New Testament quotations of the Old Testament, perhaps as many as three hundred, come from the Septuagint. The Septuagint was also used extensively in the early church. Although the New Testament writers were not ignorant of Hebrew or the Hebrew Bible, they wrote in Greek and therefore often alluded to and quoted from the Greek Old Testament, and some of the vocabulary of the New Testament comes from the Septuagint (e.g., *parsa sarx*, "all flesh," in Luke 3:6).[14]

The abbreviation LXX most likely derives from the second century B.C. Letter of Aristeas, which is one of the writings of the pseudepigrapha. The main goal of this writing is to argue the superiority of the Septuagint over any other translations of the Old

Testament. In so doing, the letter states that seventy-two Jewish scholars, six from each of the twelve tribes of Israel (and rounded off to seventy), made a translation of the Hebrew Bible in seventy days for Ptolemy II of Egypt (285–246 B.C.) to place in the famous library in Alexandria, Egypt. Although the letter claims that the translation was uniform, accurate, and made under divine inspiration, such is not the case, and contemporary scholars view the letter as an apologetic work specifically written to enhance the status of the Septuagint.

However, the Septuagint did have an important influence on Jews and Christians. As knowledge of Greek spread throughout the ancient Near East due to the conquests of Alexander the Great, having the biblical text in a language that large groups of people could read became important. This was especially so for Jews who were dispersed and living outside of Palestine. Among them and early Christians, the popularity of the Septuagint was such that for a while it was seen as the standard form of the Old Testament. For Christians, "by the late fourth century, Augustine even demanded that Jerome use its order of books for his translation."[15]

Though initially accepted by Jewish immigrants in Alexandria and elsewhere, it eventually lost favor. Wegner notes, "It is interesting that a work which the Jewish people originally esteemed so highly should eventually be rejected and condemned by them. This drastic change came about at least partly because the Septuagint increasingly became a sacred book for Christians who used it to propagate Christian teaching. . . . Also, as the scribes began to accept the authoritative, standardized text of the Masoretic Text, the Septuagint, which was not based upon this text, was necessarily condemned."[16]

Important manuscripts of the Septuagint include Codex Vaticanus, Codex Sinaiticus, Codex Alexandrinus, the Chester Beatty Papyri, the Rylands Papyri, and the Oxyrhynchus Papyri. "More manuscripts of the Greek Old Testament survive than any other ancient Greek text except the New Testament. Counting both complete and fragmentary manuscripts, nearly 2,000 handwritten copies of the Septuagint have survived."[17]

Although it is not a large part of the experience of Christians in the West, the Septuagint remains significant in Eastern Orthodox churches (Greek, Russian, and Syrian), where it was traditionally considered inspired (though that is debated in Orthodoxy today).[18]

49. What is the Vulgate?

The Vulgate (literally "common" or "plain") is a late-fourth-century A.D. Latin translation of the Bible that was primarily the work of Jerome (ca. 347–420), a scholar born in Dalmatia who studied in Rome, Damascus, and Bethlehem. Jerome's knowledge of Latin, Greek, and Hebrew, as well as his diligence in biblical study, made him the right person for such an undertaking.

Many languages were in use throughout the Roman Empire, but after the third century A.D., in Rome and on the Italian peninsula, Latin became the dominant language of religion and philosophy, supplanting Greek. As a result, there was a need by Christian writers and theologians for a Latin Bible. The Latin Vulgate filled that need.

Elsewhere in the Roman Empire, in places such as Southern Gual and North Africa, Latin had already been prevalent, and Latin copies existed of all the books of the Bible. These books, written in what is called Old Latin, were known as Old Latin Versions, a collective term used to distinguish them from the Latin Vulgate of Jerome. We know that Latin biblical texts existed in Carthage in North Africa around A.D. 150, and church fathers such as Tertullian (ca. A.D. 160–220), Cyprian (ca. A.D. 200–258), and later, Augustine of Hippo (A.D. 354–430) used such texts. They were translated into Latin from the Greek Septuagint (LXX), but after Jerome's Vulgate gained dominance, these earlier Old Latin biblical texts were not preserved, and what we know of them comes to us from quotes in the writings of the Latin church fathers.[19]

Pope Damasus I, the bishop of Rome from about 366–384,

commissioned his secretary, Jerome, to revise and standardize the existing Old Latin version of the four gospels. Over time, this endeavor grew to encompass the whole Bible, and Jerome's translation work lasted from A.D. 383 to about 405.

Jerome translated the Old Testament from Hebrew manuscripts. Textual scholar Ernst Würthwein describes the significance of Jerome's contribution: "The work which represents the real achievement of Jerome, establishing his significance for the history of the text and exercising the broadest influence for the history of Western culture, is his translation of the Old Testament from the Hebrew text which he accomplished in the years 390–405. He alone among the Christians in the West was capable of making his translation from the original text, because of his knowledge of Hebrew."[20]

Jerome learned Hebrew in Syria and in Bethlehem. In Bethlehem, he was taught by a rabbi, who visited at night for fear that other Jews would condemn him for teaching the sacred language to a Gentile.[21]

Over several centuries, Jerome's work became the accepted translation for worship, reading, and study. In Würthwein's words, "At the beginning of the seventh century it was on par with the Old Latin in the esteem and usage of the church, but in the eighth and ninth centuries it won the lead."[22] A revision was made by Alcuin (730/737–804), who was close to Charlemagne, and his revision helped make the Vulgate the standard text of France. Later in the Middle Ages, another revision known as the Paris Bible became influential, and it was in this recension that the books of the Bible were divided into chapters according to a system devised by Stephen Langton (d. 1228), a teacher in Paris and later Archbishop of Canterbury.[23]

Throughout these centuries, phrases and words of the Vulgate permeated all areas of culture and worship, inspiring liturgy, prayer, art, architecture, and music. It was the only Bible translation that most people knew or heard. By the thirteenth century, Jerome's work had come to be called the *versio vulgate*—that is, the "commonly used translation"—and ultimately it became the definitive and officially promulgated Latin version of the Bible in the Roman Catholic Church. It was decreed to be such at the Council of Trent on April 8, 1546.

During the Protestant Reformation, the Bible was translated into vernacular language of the people from the original languages of Greek and Hebrew, but also from the Latin Vulgate, and the Vulgate was often used in theological writings and debates of the Reformers. For example, the Vulgate is used and referenced in both the published Latin sermons of John Calvin and the Greek New Testament editions of Theodore Beza.

The Latin Vulgate is important in the history of the Bible in part because of its dominance and longevity in Western Europe. For more than a thousand years, it was the Bible that was used in the West. Even today, one can detect the influence of the Latin Vulgate in the development of English theological and biblical terms. Many such terms used today come from Latin words in the Vulgate and are used nearly unchanged in their meaning or spelling. Among those words are:

- *creatio* (Gen. 1:1; Heb. 9:11)
- *salvatio* (Isa. 37:32; Eph. 2:5)
- *justificatio* (Rom. 4:25; Heb. 9:1)
- *publicanus* (Matt. 10:3)
- *regeneratio* (Matt. 19:28)
- *testamentum* (Matt. 26:28)
- *sanctificatio* (1 Cor. 1:30; 1 Peter 1:2)
- *raptura* (from a noun form of the verb *rapiemur* in 1 Thess. 4:17)

Today there are more than 10,000 manuscript copies of the Latin Vulgate dating as far back as the fifth and sixth centuries. The earliest existing copy of the entire Latin Vulgate is known as Codex Amiatinus and was made in Northumbria, the northern part of England, in the eighth century. For the history of the English Bible, the Latin Vulgate is important because it was used by Oxford

University scholar John Wycliffe (1329–1384) for translation into English in the fourteenth century in what was the first English translation of the entire Bible.

50. What is the Peshitta?

The Peshitta is a version of the Old Testament translated from Hebrew into what is known as Old Syriac. The exact origin of the Old Testament translation is unknown, and there have been competing theories regarding its beginnings. In the words of Old Testament textual scholar Ernst Würthwein, "The literary problem of the Peshitta is rather complex and suffers from the lack of a critical edition describing the manuscript tradition."[24]

We do know that this version originated in the first to second centuries A.D. The Peshitta (literally, "simple," "plain," or "common") was translated by either Jews or Christians. It likely was of first-century Jewish origin, coming from Adiabene, an ancient Assyrian independent kingdom in Mesopotamia east of the Tigris River in the region of modern Iraq. From about A.D. 40–70, Adiabene's rulers converted to Judaism from Ashurism, the polytheistic religion of the Assyro-Babylonian region. When these leaders converted, they need a version of the Old Testament, especially the Pentateuch, in their own language of Syriac. That version was likely the beginning of the Peshitta.[25]

Since the fifth century A.D., when the New Testament Peshitta (translated from Greek) was completed, the Peshitta has been the official Bible for the Syriac Orthodox Church. Although the Peshitta varies in the nature of its translation, sometimes being a paraphrase and other times a literal translation, it is an important source for textual critics. The oldest complete copy of the Peshitta in existence today dates from the seventh century A.D., and a partial copy dates from the fifth century A.D.

The importance of the Peshitta to the history of the Bible is that, as a translation, it provides an early secondary witness to the reliability of the Old Testament text that is accepted and used today.

51. What are the Aramaic Targums?

By the time the return of the Jews from exile in Babylon commenced in 538 B.C., Aramaic had become the official language of the western Persian Empire and was used in daily language throughout the Near East. Hebrew was still spoken and understood, but it became common practice in the synagogues to combine the Scripture lessons that were read in Hebrew with a translation into Aramaic. The translating was called *targem*, and the translation or explanation, *Turgum* (cf. Neh. 8:8). The translations were done orally in the worship service, and eventually they came to be written and preserved. Besides translations, the Targums (*Targumim*) also provided interpretations of the biblical text.

The writing of the Targums was a gradual process, but Targums were extant before the time of Christ.[26]

Targums exist for all the books of the Hebrew Bible except Ezra, Nehemiah, and Daniel. Once newer Targums were written, earlier ones were abandoned, until eventually, after A.D. 100, two authoritative Targums emerged: Targum Onqelos and Targum Jonathan (also known as the Targum of the Prophets). Targum Onqelos dates from the second to fifth centuries A.D. It contains the Pentateuch and is the most literal of the Targums. Since at least the Middle Ages, it has been considered the most authoritative of the Targums. Targum Jonathan contains material from the books of the prophets of the Old Testament and, like Targum Onqelos, most likely dates from the second to fifth centuries A.D. Talmudic tradition attributes its authorship to Jonathan ben Uzziel, the most famous pupil of the great Jewish scholar Hillel the Elder.

There are also two Targums among the manuscripts of the Dead Sea Scrolls found at Qumran: a targum of Job (11QtgJob) which dates from the first century B.C. to first century A.D., and a Targum of Leviticus (4QtgLev) which dates from the second century B.C.

The importance of the Targums for the history of biblical text is at least threefold: some of the Targums contain translations of the biblical text; they include early Jewish traditions regarding the interpretation of the biblical texts; and they are written in Aramaic, which is closely related to biblical Hebrew. Of their significance, textual scholar Paul D. Wegner writes: "The Targums also add greatly to our understanding of how the Jews interpreted Scripture in the first to third centuries. It is even possible that some New Testament quotations come from Jewish Targums."[27] Like the Syriac Peshitta, the Septuagint, the Latin Vulgate, and the Samaritan Pentateuch, Targums are an important secondary witness to the Hebrew text of the Old Testament. Targums are understood today technically as commentaries on biblical books with some containing translations and paraphrases of the text.[28]

52. What is the Samaritan Pentateuch?

The Samaritan Pentateuch is a Hebrew version of the first five books of the Old Testament. It is written in an early Paleo-Hebrew script, unlike the square Hebrew script that arose after the post-exilic Jewish experience with Aramaic. This version of the Pentateuch is the biblical text used by the Samaritans, whose existence came about during the Babylonian exile of the Jews. The Samaritans had no relation to the Jews and knew only the Pentateuch, not the writings of the pre-exilic prophets. Their biblical history is recorded in 2 Kings 17:24–29. The Jews regarded them as half-pagan syncretists and rejected them with great animosity. In part, this was due to the Samaritan belief that the true place of worship was Mount Gerazim rather than at the Jewish Temple in Jerusalem (cf. John 4:20).

During the ministry of Jesus Christ, there were three Samaritans whose actions were recorded in the Gospels and commended by Jesus:

- "The Good Samaritan" (Luke 10:25–37) showed exceeding kindness by doing as much as he possibly could to help someone who was in need.

- "The Samaritan Leper" (Luke 17:11–19), when he realized he was healed, immediately went to Jesus and gave thanks, becoming an example of gratitude.
- "The Samaritan Woman at the Well" (John 4:1–42) listened to Jesus, believed what He told her, and then went to tell others about Him.

The composition date of the Samaritan Pentateuch is between the fifth and second centuries, with most scholars arguing for the later date, after the destruction of the Samaritan temple on Mount Gerazim in 128 B.C. by the Jewish leader John Hyrcanus.[29] In recent history, the Samaritan Pentateuch first became known to the West in 1616 through the discovery and purchase of a manuscript in Damascus by an Italian traveler, Pietro della Valle (1586–1652). The earliest and most complete version of the Samaritan Pentateuch in existence is known as the Ashiba Scroll, dating to about A.D. 1150. The scroll is owned by the Samaritan community of Nablus, or biblical Shechem, a city in the northern West Bank about thirty-nine miles north of Jerusalem.

While there is substantial agreement between the Samaritan Pentateuch and the Masoretic Text, there are about 6,000 minor variations, mostly orthographic and not affecting the meaning of the text. Some of the variations are intentional alterations, such as a command inserted after Exodus 20:17 to build a sanctuary at Mount Gerazim.[30]

The importance of the Samaritan Pentateuch in the history of the biblical text lies in the explanatory notes that accompany it and help textual critics understand the history of the textual transmission. For instance, there are manuscripts from the Dead Sea Scrolls that have writings in agreement with biblical verses. These manuscripts, in addition to agreement in other texts such as some in the Septuagint show that there was widespread knowledge and use of the Samaritan Pentateuch.[31]

PART 9

The Interpretation of the Bible[1]

53. Is there more than one meaning in a biblical text?

An established rule for interpreting a literary document is that every statement has only one meaning. Years ago, Milton Terry, in his book *Biblical Hermeneutics*, said, "A fundamental principle in grammatico-historical exposition is that the words and sentences can have but one significance in one and the same connection. The moment we neglect this principle we drift out upon a sea of uncertainty and conjecture."[2]

The meaning of a given text, whether it is a biblical book, a Supreme Court ruling, or a letter to a friend, is the meaning that is in the mind of the author. On the other hand, interpretation is in the mind of the reader. Only when the interpreter is able to connect his interpretation with the author's intended meaning does correct interpretation occur.

The Difference Between Meaning and Interpretation[3]

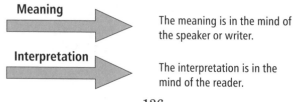

Meaning

The meaning is in the mind of the speaker or writer.

Interpretation

The interpretation is in the mind of the reader.

Part of the confusion regarding the number of meanings in a given text relates to interchanging the words *meaning* and *interpretation*, and *meaning* and *significance*. Let us look at this for a moment.

Maybe you have been in a Bible study in which the leader asks each person to read a verse of a passage being studied and tell the group what it means to him or her. This is the wrong question. Until a person discovers what a passage meant to its author, the significance of that passage for the reader is uncertain. We must first determine what the author actually meant by the words that he chose and the context in which he wrote the words. We have no moral right to give a new meaning to what the inspired writer wrote. After we have determined the meaning, then we ask, how does this passage relate to my life? How do I apply this text? These questions relate to the implications of the meaning intended by the author. There may be many implications or applications, but only one meaning, and we must not put the cart before the horse if we are to be accurate and faithful interpreters of the words of God.

What is application? We define it as the extension of the meaning in the text to a situation in life that is consistent with the meaning of the text. Consequently, the application must not stray from the meaning of the author in the text being interpreted. For example, in Galatians 3:28, Paul says that all have equal access to the spiritual benefits of Christ found within the Abrahamic covenant (Gen. 12:3) by faith in Christ, whether they be Jew or Greek, slave or free, male or female, because we are all one in Christ. The apostle's meaning is that distinctions between people do not affect the oneness that believers have in Christ; all are children of Abraham by faith. Are the groups in Paul's list the only ones he could have mentioned? No. If asked whether being black or white breaks this unity of the faithful, Paul would say no. If asked whether being rich or poor breaks this unity, he would respond no. The specific meaning, illustrated by Jew or Greek, slave or free, male or female, may be extended to black or white and rich or poor. Thus, the application is the meaning extended to a new situation that is consistent with the original meaning. Some have used this passage to teach that offices and functions in the church are open to all distinctions of people, but this is disparate from the meaning intended in the text.

The Difference Between Meaning and Implication[4]

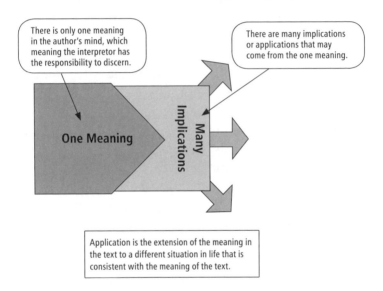

There is only one meaning in the author's mind, which meaning the interpretor has the responsibility to discern.

There are many implications or applications that may come from the one meaning.

One Meaning

Many Implications

Application is the extension of the meaning in the text to a different situation in life that is consistent with the meaning of the text.

54. What is figurative language?

Both literal language and figurative language may be used to express a literal truth (in contrast to an allegory or spiritualization). What is called *plain-literal interpretation*, or normal interpretation, refers to the *denotative* meaning in a given text—that is, the face value of the words. What is called *figurative-literal* also is used to convey a literal truth, but by means of *connotative* language. In this case, one must discover the specific intention of the figure of speech used to express a literal truth.

The search for literal truth, in contradistinction from allegorical truth, includes the use of figures of speech, with the understanding that behind every figure of speech is a literal meaning. The literal meaning is the natural or plain meaning of the figure of speech and is a means by which the author seeks to convey his meaning. There are never two senses, one literal and one figurative, as is the case with allegory.

There is nothing wrong with using figures of speech, since they often accentuate or intensify a meaning. For example, Jesus is called the Lion of the tribe of Judah, a more picturesque and powerful way of conveying the sense that He is a strong ruler. John the Baptist's words, "Behold the Lamb of God who takes away the sin of the world," is more expressive than saying, "Behold the One who is meek and will take away the sin of the world," because the weakness and meekness of the lamb as a sin-bearer in that culture had much history in the sacrificial lamb and the scapegoat. Consequently, figurative language does not diminish accuracy but actually enhances it.

The Distinction Between Literal and Figurative Language in Determining Literal Truth[5]

Plain-Literal Language	Figurative-Literal Language
Denotative: The literal interpretation is the explicit assertion of the words.	Connotative: The literal interpretation is the specific intention of the figure of speech. A connotative statement is one that expresses a literal truth by using a figure of speech.

As much as figurative language can help to express meaning (provided it is correctly understood by the interpreter), some guidelines nevertheless need to be observed in working with it. First, do not build doctrine on figurative language. Go to a similar passage that deals with the same material or topic in a plain-literal sense.

Second, find out what the writer means when he uses a particular figure of speech. Often the author will use the same figure in the same way throughout his writing.

Third, look for the plain-literal meaning first, for it is more common. For example, in Zechariah 14:4, the text indicates that the Messiah will stand on the Mount of Olives in the last days, and the mountain will split in two, from east to west, making a large valley. There is no reason to doubt the literal sense of the passage. Jesus stood on the Mount of Olives in His first coming, and there is no reason to believe the passage should mean anything other than the denotative sense.

Fourth, one should never depart from the plain-literal interpretation unless the context of the passage provides good reason to do so. A challenge to one's theological system is not sufficient reason to depart from the plain-literal interpretation.

Fifth, look for an explanation of the figure in its context. For example, in John 7:37, Jesus said that if anyone thirsted, he should come to Jesus, and out of this person would flow rivers of water. John then explained that Jesus meant the person would receive the Holy Spirit.

You should look for a figurative expression if the plain-literal means involves an inherent contradiction with other Scripture or with general facts, or if there is a physical or moral impossibility involved, of if the meaning is contradicted by the context of the passage.

Last of all, the old adage is still true: "When the Scripture makes sense, seek no other sense, lest it be nonsense."

55. What is meant by "literal interpretation"?

When we say that one should generally understand the biblical text in a literal way, we mean that a plain, non-figurative reading of the text is the norm. You should only view the text as metaphorical or figurative if it compels you to do so. Texts written in a figurative manner can be largely incomprehensible. The figure is placed among non-figurative ideas to add color, to enhance, but if figures are used too much, the text will lack clarity. Bear in mind that both denotative and connotative expressions lead to literal truth in Scripture.

One follows a literal interpretive approach by use of the grammatical-historical-cultural-contextual method. This means that you will look at the words of a passage in their context, both grammatically and lexicographically (that is, determining word meanings), and you will consider how the culture and history behind the passage influenced the way it was understood by its author and original recipients.

Figurative language is especially used in poetry and prophecy in the Scripture. The literal interpreter is not one who denies that figurative language is used in prophecy. He only argues that prophetic utterances must be understood as any other utterances are interpreted. Whatever is manifestly literal should be regarded as plain-literal, and what is manifestly figurative should be considered figurative-literal. Again, however, both kinds of interpretation should lead to one meaning: the literal one, not an allegory.

The Process of Interpretation[6]

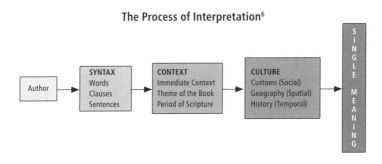

PART 10

Contemporary Challenges Regarding the Bible

56. Are books missing from the Bible today?

The history of the Scriptures involves not only the books that were approved as canonical, but also many that were purposely excluded. Some were not included in the Old Testament, and an even greater number were left out of the New Testament. The excluded texts are called the Apocrypha and pseudepigrapha.

To some extent, most people are familiar with the Apocrypha. These books were written between 200 B.C. and A.D. 100. They are helpful books that describe with considerable accuracy the religious, political, and social conditions of the years between the Old and New Testaments. However, none of them were ever included in the Hebrew Bible, and neither Christ nor the New Testament writers ever cited from the Apocrypha, whereas they quoted liberally from the Old Testament. Additionally, with few exceptions, all of the lists of canonical books in the first four centuries of the church omit these books.

The Apocrypha contains doctrinal errors (such as the justification of suicide and prayers for the dead), historical errors, and folklore and myths, all of which makes them impossible to accept as inspired by God. Moreover, unlike the Old and New Testaments, none of the books claim to have been inspired or to have been written by a prophet or apostle.

The second category of excluded books is the pseudepigrapha, a name given to a large number of Jewish and pseudo-Christian writings produced between 200 B.C. and A.D. 200. The term *pseudepigrapha* means "false writing." Some of the Old Testament books claim to have been written by Adam, Enoch, Moses, and Ezra, and New Testament books by Barnabas, Peter, Thomas, and Paul. In addition to false claims of authorship, many of these books have considerable fanciful content, and some contain blatant false teaching.

On the other hand, some of the pseudepigrapha are quite helpful in understanding how early Jews and Christians understood the theology of the Bible. Two of these books, Enoch and the Assumption of Moses, are quoted by the writer Jude, and later by such important church fathers as Irenaeus.

The pseudepigrapha were never included in the Canon. Many were largely heretical and fanciful, and many were representative of Gnostic views. None of them met the stringent tests of canonicity.

57. Does the Bible quote from other ancient writings?

Two authors of Scripture quote from works outside the Bible, namely, Paul and Jude. The apostle Paul, in his defense before the philosophers on the Aeropagus in Athens, quotes from at least two pagan poets and may have alluded to others. Moreover, Jude quotes from two works, the Book of Enoch and the Assumption of Moses.

Does this mean that the authors of Scripture considered these works to be inspired and that they should be included in the canon of Scripture? No. Neither Paul nor Jude represented them in that light, and the church never entertained the notion that they should be in the Canon.

There is little doubt that writers of Scripture, and most certainly the church fathers, referred to other works that were not inspired books, even as we do today. But neither they nor most of us today consider the non-canonical books to be the Word of God. They provide much helpful information, and surely much of what they say is true. Truth resides outside of Scripture. But what the Scripture affirms is in fact faithful to God's perspective of reality.

Examine the following chart for a comparison of Paul's and Jude's statements in which they quote from non-canonical sources.

Non-Canonical Sources Referred to by Paul and Jude in the New Testament[1]	
Paul in Acts 17:22–31	
Paul's Statement	*Similar Idea from Pagan Literature*
17:22 "So Paul stood in the midst of the Areopagus and said, 'Men of Athens, I observe that you are **very religious in all respects**.'"	"This city (Athens) **goes beyond all in worshipping and reverencing the gods**." **Soph**. *Oepid. Colon.* V.1006.
17:23 "For while I was passing through and examining the objects of your worship, I also found an altar with this inscription, 'TO AN **UNKNOWN GOD**.'"	"Let us adore **the Unknown** at Athens, stretching forth our hands towards heaven." **Lucian**, *Philop.* c. 29.
17:25 "nor is He served by human hands, **as though He needed anything**, since He Himself gives to all *people* life and breath and all things."	"The Deity, if he be truly deity, **lacks nothing**." **Eurip**. *Herc. fur.* v.1345. "God is **absolutely exempt from wants**. . ." **Plut**. *Comp. Arist.* c. Caton. c.4.
17:28 "for in Him we live and move and exist, as even some of your own poets have said, '**For we also are His children**.'"	"The first generations of men were of a noble spirit; and, if I may so speak, the immediate **offspring of the gods**." **Senec**. *epist*. 90. "We feel his spirit moving here, and everywhere. And **we his offspring are**." **Arat**. *Phaen.* v1. "For mortals all, Thee to address is meet; For **we are thy offspring**." **Cleanth**. *Hymn. in Jov.*

7:29 "Being then the children of God, **we ought not to think that the Divine Nature is like gold or silver** or stone, an image formed by the art and thought of man."	"**Do you suppose I mean** some god without you, **of gold or silver?**" *Epict.* 1.II.c.8. "Rise then, and show yourself worthy of the Deity; **a god not made of gold or silver**; for of such materials it is indeed impossible to form a likeness of God." **Senec.** *epist.* 31.

Jude in Verses 9 and 14–15	
9 "But Michael the archangel, when he disputed with the devil and argued about the body of Moses, did not dare pronounce against him a railing judgment, but said, 'The Lord rebuke you!'"	This particular portion quoted by Jude is no longer extant but has been reproduced in the writings of the church fathers Clement of Alexandria, Origen, and Didymus. Their accounts, when pieced together, present the archangel Michael in conflict with the devil over the body of Moses, at which time Michael says to the devil, "The Lord rebuke you." See the discussion on this difficult reconstruction by R. H. Charles, ed., *The Assumption of Moses* (London: Adam and Charles Black, 1897), 105–110.

14–15 "It *was* also about these men that **Enoch**, *in* the seventh *generation* from Adam, prophesied, saying, 'Behold, the Lord came with many thousands of His holy ones, to execute judgment upon all, and to convict all the ungodly of all their ungodly deeds which they have done in an ungodly way, and of all the harsh things which ungodly sinners have spoken against Him.'"	**Enoch** 1:9
	"Look, he comes with the myriads of his
	   holy ones,
	to execute judgment on all,
	and to destroy the wicked,
	and to convict all humanity
	   for all the wicked deeds that they
	     have done,
	   and the proud and hard words that
	     wicked sinners spoke against him."
	
	George W. E. Nickelsburg and James C. VanderKam, *1 Enoch: A New Translation* (Minneapolis: Fortress, 2004), 20.

58. What is the relationship of the Dead Sea Scrolls to the Bible?

The Dead Sea Scrolls are one of the greatest archaeological discoveries in history.[2] They are a collection of scrolls and fragments of scrolls that first came to public awareness in 1947 and were announced internationally in headlines in 1948. They were discovered in late 1946 or early 1947 by an Arab shepherd boy in caves that dot the cliffs along the western shore of the Dead Sea in Israel. He was throwing rocks in one of the caves to see if a goat had wandered inside and heard a rock hit a piece of pottery. When he later went inside to investigate, he found the broken pottery containing manuscripts. Other manuscripts were buried in the floors of the caves.

The Dead Sea Scrolls provide information about various issues and concerns of Jews during the New Testament era. There are thousands of small fragments of scrolls and numerous scrolls or portions of scrolls containing more than 900 texts and portions of texts from the Hebrew Bible, non-canonical books, and writings related to the Jewish sect that lived at Qumran, the location of the caves. When the caves were excavated by archaeologists, they found that at least eleven caves contained more than 400 manuscripts. When collated, these represented all the books of the Old Testament (often with multiple copies) except Esther and Nehemiah. The scrolls and manuscripts found in the caves are dated from about 250 B.C. to A.D. 50—years before and during the life of Jesus and the early New Testament era.

The Dead Sea Scrolls are extremely important for biblical studies and the history of the Bible, especially the Old Testament. Scrolls expert Craig A. Evans notes, "It is hard to overestimate the significance of the [Dead Sea Scrolls] for biblical studies. The scrolls probably constitute the single most important manuscript find in history. There have been other important finds, such as the Nag Hammadi manuscripts found in the desert sands of Egypt, but no other find has had more importance for understanding the Bible and the world of Jesus and his earliest followers."[3]

Evans shows that there are eight ways the scrolls help us to better understand the Bible:

1. They provide information and insight into the study of ancient writing and the process of making scrolls.
2. They provide confirmation of the text of the Hebrew portion of the Bible (for Christians, the Old Testament).
3. They provide insights into the languages of Hebrew and Aramaic as they were used in the time of Jesus.
4. They provide some new writings that resemble the Old Testament but were written later and falsely attributed to biblical authors.
5. They provide examples of how the Bible was interpreted more than 2,000 years ago.
6. They provide information on the social and cultural environments of Jesus and early Christianity.
7. They provide better understanding of Jewish teachings and beliefs during the time of Jesus.
8. They provide background information regarding the Jewish background of Jesus and the New Testament.[4]

Until the scrolls were found, the oldest complete Hebrew manuscript of the Old Testament was the text of Codex Leningradensis, dated to 1008–1009 (though portions of the Old Testament in a manuscript known as the Aleppo Codex date from a century earlier). What the Dead Sea Scrolls did was push back the date of extant manuscripts a thousand years. It made the earliest extant copies of books of the Old Testament much closer to the dates of the original texts. It also created the ability to compare Hebrew texts of the Old Testament and confirm that what we now use is the same text as in the Dead Sea Scrolls, with only minimal differences. If we look at the Dead Sea Scrolls, the medieval manuscripts from about A.D. 800 to 1000, and the Hebrew texts of today, the text is the same, with only minor exceptions. The accuracy of the Old Testament text was thus affirmed.

Most New Testament scholars agree that there are no New Testament documents among the Dead Sea Scrolls. (Two scholars believe that Cave 7 has a fragment of Mark 6; however, this notion is almost universally rejected.) The inhabitants of the Qumran community were a very legalistic Jewish sect and hostile to Christians and even others Jews, so there is no reason to expect New Testament documents among them. Additionally, the Qumran community was destroyed in A.D. 68, and while much of the New Testament was finished by then, it is unlikely that copies would have circulated beyond Christian circles. Rather than being New Testament writings, the fragments from Cave 7 are very likely from the Jewish book of Enoch.[5]

Some of the scrolls refer to a coming Messiah, and although Jesus is not identified in the scrolls as the long-awaited Messiah, there are parallels in the scrolls that shed light on the life and ministry of Jesus Christ. For example, the Rule of the Congregation Scroll (1QSa) tells of a future day when the Messiah will sit at a banquet with Israel's elders: "This is the procedure for the meeting of the men of repute when they are called to the banquet held by the Council of the Community, when God has begotten the Messiah among them" (1QSa 2:11–12).[6]

There are also similar words and attitudes between the beatitudes of Jesus (Matt. 5:3–12) and fragments of a scroll known at 4Q525. And there are differences as well.[7]

The scrolls are very helpful in understanding the world of Jesus and the New Testament. As supplemental material to the Bible and in the field of biblical studies, they are exciting and valuable. They provide clarification and insight into prophetic and messianic expectations of the first century, and in so doing show the reasonableness of the writings of the Bible. But "the scrolls neither make nor break the Christian faith."[8]

59. How do early copies of the Bible compare with early copies of other ancient literature?

Compared to other ancient and classical pieces of literature, there are far more partial and complete manuscripts of the Old Testament and New Testament than any of the other writings. Additionally, the gap between the date of the original writing and the earliest copy of the original manuscript is a little over a century, and perhaps much less in the case of Mark.[9]

New Testament scholar F. F. Bruce writes of the comparison with the manuscripts of the New Testament: "The evidence for our New Testament writings is ever so much greater than the evidence for many writings of classical authors, the authenticity of which no one dreams of questioning. And if the New Testament were a collection of secular writings, their authenticity would generally be regarded as beyond all doubt."[10]

Comparison of Manuscripts of Ancient Literature and the New Testament[11]						
Author	Book	Date Written	Earliest Copies	Time Gap	Number of Copies	Accuracy
Homer	Illiad	ca. 850 B.C.	ca. 400 B.C.	450 years	1,900	95%
Herodotus	History	ca. 480– 425 B.C.	ca. A.D. 900	1,350 years	8	Too few to determine
Thucydides	History	460– 400 B.C.	ca. A.D. 900	1,400 years	8	Too few to determine
Euripedes	Various plays	440 B.C.	ca. A.D. 1100	1,500 years	9	Too few to determine
Plato	Various	ca. 400 B.C.	ca. A.D. 900	1,300 years	7	Reconstructed texts
Demos-thenes	Various	300 B.C.	ca. A.D. 1100	1,400 years	200	Reconstructed texts
Caesar	Gallic Wars	58– 44 B.C.	ca. A.D. 900	1,000 years	20	Reconstructed texts

continued . . .

Comparison of Manuscripts of Ancient Literature and the New Testament *continued*						
Author	Book	Date Written	Earliest Copies	Time Gap	Number of Copies	Accuracy
Catallus	Various poems	ca. 50 B.C.	ca. A.D. 1500	1,500 years	3	Too few to determine
Tacitus	*Annals*	ca. A.D. 100	ca. A.D. 1100	1,000 years	20	Reconstructed texts
Livy	*History of Rome*	ca. 37 B.C.– A.D. 17	Partial A.D. 4th c., mostly 10th c.	400–1,000 years	1 partial; 19 copies	Reconstructed texts
Pliny	*Natural History*	ca. A.D. 70	ca. A.D. 850	780 years	7	Too few to determine
New Testament		ca. A.D. 40–95	ca. A.D. 114 (fragment) ca. 200 (books) ca. 250 (most of NT) ca. 325 (complete NT)	50 years 100 years 150 years 225 years	Approx. 5,700	99.5%

60. Is the Bible a sufficient guide for what we believe and how we live?

The Bible contains all the words that God intended for us to have and all that we need to know from God about salvation, trusting God, and obeying God. It does not tell us everything that we want to know, but everything that we need to know (2 Tim. 3:15–16; James 1:18; 1 Peter 1:23). We can be sure that in the pages of the Bible, the information we find about doctrine and life is true and is all that we need to know about such subjects. We do not need to search for additional revelation from God. In the Bible, we will be able to find exactly what God wants us to know about these topics. God is not adding new revelation. He has given us what we need.

When we have concerns or questions about life and doctrine, we can find what we need in the pages of the Bible.

Either directly or indirectly, the Bible speaks to every area of life. Sometimes it is through commandments, both positive and negative; sometimes through principles; sometimes through illustrations; and sometimes through doctrine. But it is all there, and it will aid us in skillful and godly living if we will look to the Bible's content. The sufficiency of Scripture means that we are not to add to or detract from Scripture, and no other writing is to be considered as of equal value. We are not required to believe anything about God that is not found in the Bible.

Conclusion

God has spoken. He is not silent. In the pages of the Bible, there is sure and certain guidance from God to all who will read or listen to its words. It contains a message for the many, the few, and you. God loves you and sent His Son, Jesus Christ, to earth to die for your sins and to offer you eternal life if you will believe (John 3:16).

Directly or indirectly, the Bible is applicable to every area of life. The more you read it, the more you will understand it. Don't be put off by passages you don't understand. Rather, keep reading and studying. If you do, you will be surprised by how clear and insightful the Bible will become for you.

Theologian Carl F. H. Henry astutely wrote in a national press article, "The Bible is still the most incisive critic of our age. It confronts our broken love of God, our dull sense of justice, our shameful moral nakedness, our waning sense of ethical duty, our badly numbed consciences, our clutching anxieties, the ghastly horrors and brutal violence of this era."[1]

He was right. The Bible is the best critic and guide for this age, and every age, that is available to us.

The longest psalm in the book of Psalms is Psalm 119. Its 176 verses extol God's revelation to humanity found in the Scriptures. In verse 105, the psalmist declares, "Your word is a lamp to my feet and a light to my path." We encourage you to use the Bible as just that—a guide for all of life as you journey through the years. Read it. You will not be disappointed. It is the most important book you will ever read.

Notes

Part 1: The Origin of the Bible

1. Some conservatives who date the Exodus from 1290 B.C. would consider the period to be 1,300 years.

2. H. Wayne House and Timothy J. Demy, "Authorship and Dating of Old Testament Books," http://christianperspective international.com/publications/charts.html; © 2011 H. Wayne House and Timothy Demy. All rights reserved.

3. Randall Price, *Searching for the Original Bible* (Eugene, OR: Harvest House, 2007), 88–89.

4. Paul D. Wegner, *The Journey from Texts to Translations: The Origin and Development of the Bible* (Grand Rapids: Baker, 1999), 82.

5. On the role of memorization in the era, see Birger Gerhardsson, *Memory and Manuscript with Tradition and Transmission in Early Christianity* (Grand Rapids: Eerdmans, 1998). Richard Bauckham, *Jesus and the Eyewitnesses: The Gospel as Eyewitness Testimony* (Grand Rapids: Eerdmans, 2006), 249–52, notes that Gerhardsson's work is not without weaknesses, though some of the criticisms directed against it are due to misunderstanding and misrepresentation by its critics. On the use of the Septuagint in the Gospels and Acts, see Karen H. Jobes and Moisés Silva, *Invitation to the Septuagint* (Grand Rapids: Baker, 2000), 193–95.

6. On Aramaic Targums, see Wegner, *Journey from Texts to*

Translations, 202–204; and B. H. Young, "Targum," in *The International Standard Bible Encyclopedia*, ed. Geoffrey W. Bromily (Grand Rapids: Eerdmans, 1988), 4:727–33.

7. Gleason L. Archer and G. C. Chirichigno, *Old Testament Quotations in the New Testament: A Complete Survey* (Chicago: Moody Press, 1983), ix. On the intricacies of the use of the Old Testament in the New Testament, see Kenneth Berding and Jonathan Lunde, eds., *Three Views on the New Testament Use of the Old Testament* (Grand Rapids: Zondervan, 2008).

8. Johnston M. Cheney, *The Life of Christ in Stereo: The Four Gospels Combined as One*, ed. Stanley A. Ellisen (Portland, OR: Western Baptist Seminary Press, 1969).

Part 2: The Organization of the Bible

1. Walter C. Kaiser Jr., *The Old Testament Documents: Are They Reliable and Relevant?* (Westmont, IL: InterVarsity, 2001), 33–34.

2. Ibid., 35–36.

3. Paul D. Wegner, *The Journey from Texts to Translations: The Origin and Development of the Bible* (Grand Rapids: Baker, 1999), 60–61.

4. For more on the arrangement of New Testament books, see Arthur G. Patzia, *The Making of the New Testament: Origin, Collection, Text, and Canon*, 2nd ed. (Westmont, IL: InterVarsity, 2011), 176–83.

5. H. Wayne House and Timothy J. Demy, "Divisions of the English Bible," http://www.hwhouse.com/publications/charts.html; © 2011 H. Wayne House and Timothy J. Demy. All rights reserved.

6. Wegner, *Journey from Texts to Translations*, 176–77, 213.

7. Ibid., 214.

Part 3: The Uniqueness of the Bible

1. On this, see the important study by Richard Bauckham, *Jesus and the Eyewitnesses Testimony* (Grand Rapids: Eerdmans, 2006).

2. On the early history of Christianity and science, see James Hannam, *The Genesis of Science: How the Late Christian Middle Ages Launched the Scientific Revolution* (Washington, D.C.: Regnery, 2011); and his work *God's Philosophers: How the Medieval World Laid the Foundations of Modern Science* (London: Icon, 2010).

3. The defense of Christianity (Christian apologetics) is an enormous topic that is beyond the scope of this work. For an introduction to it, see H. Wayne House and Dennis Jowers, *Reasons for Our Hope: An Introduction to Christian Apologetics* (Nashville: B&H, 2011).

4. On this, see H. Wayne House, ed., *Intelligent Design 101: Leading Experts Explain the Key Issues* (Grand Rapids: Kregel, 2008).

5. On some of these difficult passages, see Tim Demy and Gary Stewart, *101 Most Puzzling Bible Verses* (Eugene, OR: Harvest House, 2006).

6. On the uniqueness of the Bible with respect to its composition, continuity, and history, see Josh McDowell, *The New Evidence That Demands a Verdict* (Nashville: Thomas Nelson, 1999), 3–16.

7. Charles C. Ryrie, *Basic Theology* (Colorado Springs: Victor, 1982), 71.

8. For additional information on the defense of Christianity (Christian apologetics), see House and Jowers, *Reasons for Our Hope*; and H. Wayne House and Joseph M. Holden, *Charts of Apologetics and Christian Evidences* (Grand Rapids: Zondervan, 2006).

9. Carl F. H. Henry, *Twilight of a Great Civilization* (Wheaton, IL: Crossway, 1988), 44.

10. Ryrie, *Basic Theology*, 72.

11. The material on errors in the Bible is based on H. Wayne House, *Charts of Christian Theology and Doctrine* (Grand Rapids: Zondervan, 1992), chart 12. Used by permission; and

The House Visual Study Bible (Olive Tree Bible Software, 2012; http://www.olivetree.com).

12. See Darrell L. Bock, *Luke 1:1–9:50,* Baker Exegetical Commentary of the New Testament (Grand Rapidis: Baker, 1994), 348–62, 918–24; and Bock, *Luke,* The NIV Application Commentary (Grand Rapids: Zondervan, 1996), 122–26.

13. See errors in the Gospels according to Bart Ehrman in the transcript of his debate with William Lane Craig titled "Is There Historical Evidence for the Resurrection of Jesus?," http://academics.holycross.edu/files/crec/resurrection-debate-transcript.pdf.

14. Aratus, *Phaenomena,* 1.5 trans. A. W. Mair and G. R. Mair, Loeb Classical Library (Cambridge, MA: Harvard University Press, 1921).

15. Beegle, *The Inspiration of Scripture,* 56.

16. The chart is based on a presentation of principles by Josh McDowell, *The New Evidence That Demands a Verdict,* 47. It is borrowed from H. Wayne House and Timothy J. Demy, "Principles to Use When Dealing with Alleged Errors in Scripture," http://www.hwhouse.com/publications/charts.html; © 2011 H. Wayne House and Timothy J. Demy. All rights reserved.

17. John W. Wenham, "Christ's View of Scripture," *Inerrancy,* ed. Norman L. Geisler (Grand Rapids: Zondervan, 1980), 3–36.

18. Walter C. Kaiser Jr., *The Old Testament Documents: Are They Reliable and Relevant?* (Westmont, IL: InterVarsity, 2001), 38.

19. Edwin A. Blum, "The Apostles' View of Scripture," *Inerrancy,* 39–53.

20. See Hershel Shanks, "When Did Ancient Israel Begin?" *Biblical Archaeology Review* 38, no. 1 (2012): 59–62, 67.

21. For a treatment of the historical reliability of the Old and New Testament, see House and Jowers, *Reasons for Our Hope,* 291–309.

22. Sir Frederic Kenyon, *Bible and Archaeology* (London: Harrap, 1940), 288–89.

23. A. N. Sherwin-White, *Roman Law and Roman Society in the New Testament* (Grand Rapids: Baker, 1963), 89.

24. Nelson Glueck, *Rivers in the Desert: A History of the Negev* (New York: Farrar, Strauss & Cudahy, 1959), 31.

25. William Ramsey, *The Bearing of Recent Discovery on the Trustworthiness of the New Testament* (Grand Rapids: Baker, 1953), 222.

26. William F. Albright, *The Biblical Period from Abraham to Ezra* (New York: HarperCollins, 1960), 1–2.

27. Edwin Yamauchi, *The Stones and the Scriptures* (Philadelphia: Lippincott, Williams & Wilkins, 1972), 36.

28. On reliability, see also K. A. Kitchen, *On the Reliability of the Old Testament* (Grand Rapids: Eerdmans, 2003).

Part 4: The Gospels and Acts

1. "The excessive skepticism of many liberal theologians stems not from a careful evaluation of the available data, but from an enormous predisposition against the supernatural." Millard Burrows, *What Mean These Stones?* (New York: Meridian, 1956), 176.

2. Noted scholar of Roman history and law Sherwin-White says, "For Acts the confirmation of historicity is overwhelming. Yet Acts is, in simple terms and judged externally, no less of a propaganda narrative than the Gospels, liable to similar distortions. But any attempt to reject its basic historicity even in matters of detail must now appear absurd. Roman historians have long taken it for granted." See A. N. Sherwin-White, *Roman Law and Roman Society in the New Testament* (Grand Rapids: Baker, 1963), 189.

Mediterranean archaeologist Sir William Ramsay exclaimed, "Luke is a historian of the first rank; not merely are his statements of fact trustworthy . . . [but] this author should be placed along with the very greatest of historians." See Sir W. M. Ramsay, *The Bearing of Recent Discovery on the Trust-worthiness of the New Testament* (London, Hodder & Stoughton, 1920), 222.

Also see the more recent work of Colin J. Hemer, *The Book of Acts in the Setting of Hellenistic History* (Winona Lake, IN: Eisenbrauns, 1990), in which Hemer establishes the substantial historical accuracy of Luke's work.

3. For further arguments regarding the historical reliability of the New Testament, H. Wayne House and Dennis Jowers, *Reasons for Our Hope: An Introduction to Christian Apologetics* (Nashville: B&H, 2011); and Mark D. Roberts, *Can We Trust the Gospels? Investigating the Reliability of Matthew, Mark, Luke, and John* (Wheaton, IL: Crossway, 2007).

4. See the seminal and thought-provoking study of Richard Bauckham, *Jesus and the Eyewitnesses.*

5. Robert H. Gundry, *The Use of the Old Testament in St. Matthew's Gospel* (Leiden, NL: Brill, 1967), 181–83.

6. Ralph P. Martin, *New Testament Foundations: A Guide for Christian Students*, vol. 1, *The Four Gospels* (Grand Rapids: Eerdmans, 1975), 20. See pp. 16–29 for a more complete discussion of the meaning of *gospel.*

Part 5: The Canonicity of the Bible

1. For an overview of the history and questions surrounding the Apocrypha, see Norman L. Geisler and William E. Nix, *A General Introduction to the Bible*, rev. ed. (Chicago: Moody Press, 1986), 264–75.

2. Ibid., 262–63.

3. For more information on recognition of the Canon, see Geisler and Nix, *A General Introduction to the Bible,* 221–34.

4. Bruce M. Metzger, *The Canon of the New Testament: It's Origin, Development, and Significance* (Oxford: Oxford University Press, 1987), 291.

5. Walter C. Kaiser Jr., *The Old Testament Documents: Are They Reliable and Relevant?* (Westmont, IL: InterVarsity, 2001), 36.

6. David Noel Freedman, "The Earliest Bible," in *Backgrounds for the Bible,* ed. Michael Patrick O'Connor and David Noel Freedman (Winona Lake, IN: Eisenbrauns, 1987), 29.

7. For an overview of these opposing arguments, see Randall Price, *Searching for the Original Bible* (Eugene, OR: Harvest House, 2007), 144–47. Price agrees with our view but gives a nice summary of the issue.

8. Ibid., 147.

9. Kaiser, *The Old Testament Documents*, 31.

10. Ibid.

11. Ibid., 30.

12. Ibid., 38–39.

13. Paul D. Wegner, *The Journey from Texts to Translations: The Origin and Development of the Bible* (Grand Rapids: Baker, 1999), 140–45.

14. Ibid., 145.

15. Ibid., 145–46.

16. Ibid., 144.

17. Ibid., 127.

18. Ibid., 128–29.

19. Ibid., 129.

20. Tim Demy and Gary Stewart, *101 Most Puzzling Bible Verses* (Eugene, OR: Harvest House, 2006), 205–6.

21. Ibid., 207–8.

22. For a full discussion of the Gnostic Gospels and recent debate about them, see Darrell L. Bock, *The Missing Gospels: Unearthing the Truth Behind Alternative Christianities* (Nashville: Thomas Nelson, 2006).

23. Bock, *The Missing Gospels,* 59–65, 98–100.

24. For a full discussion and response to the errors of Dan Brown and similar supporters, see Darrell L. Bock, *Breaking the Da Vinci Code* (Nashville: Thomas Nelson, 2004).

25. Patton Dodd, "Why the Gnostic Gospels Lost: An Interview with Darrell L. Bock," December 2006, http://www.beliefnet.com/Faiths/Christianity/2006/11/Why-The-Gnostic-Gospels-Lost.aspx.

26. For an overview of the contents of each of the books, see Bruce M. Metzger, "The Apocrypha and Pseudepigrapha," in ed. Frank E. Gaebelein, *The Expositor's Bible Commentary*, vol. 1, *Introductory Articles* (Grand Rapids: Zondervan, 1979), 163–70.

27. Wegner, *Journey from Texts to Translations*, 121–22.

28. Ibid., 122.

29. For an overview of the arguments for and against inclusion in the Canon, see Wegner, *Journey from Texts to Translations*, 124–27.

30. Metzger, "The Apocrypha and Pseudepigrapha," 174.

Part 6: The Composition of the Bible

1. See "The Blessing of the Silver Scrolls," *Bible and Spade* 19, no. 2 (Spring 2006), http://www.biblearchaeology.org/post/2010/01/06/The-Blessing-of-the-Silver-Scrolls.aspx#Article.

Part 7: The Transcription and Transmission of the Bible

1. Arthur G. Patzia, *The Making of the New Testament: Origin, Collection, Text, and Canon,* 2nd ed. (Westmont, IL: InterVarsity, 2011), 229.

2. On the last twelve verses of Mark, see David Alan Black, ed., *Perspectives on the Ending of Mark: Four Views* (Nashville: B&H, 2008).

3. Patzia, *Making of the New Testament*, 230–35.

4. Ibid., 235–41.

5. On the number of textual variants, see Daniel B. Wallace, "The Number of Textual Variants: An Evangelical Miscalculation," http://www.bible.org/article/number-textual-variants-evangelical-miscalculation.

6. Daniel B. Wallace, "Lost in Transmission: How Badly Did the Scribes Corrupt the New Testament Text?" in Daniel B. Wallace, ed., *Revisiting the Corruption of the New Testament: Manuscript, Patristic, and Apocryphal Evidence* (Grand Rapids: Kregel, 2011), 55.

7. H. Wayne House and Timothy J. Demy, "The Geographical Centers of New Testament Text Types," http://www.hwhouse .com/publications/charts.html; © 2011 H. Wayne House and Timothy J. Demy. All rights reserved. Permission to use Accordance for creation of map given by OakTree Software, Inc.

8. This last item concerning orthodoxy needs to be considered and applied with great caution. Philip Miller rightly concludes that "the least orthodox reading, by itself, is *not* a viable canon for determining the preferred reading," p. 89 in Philip M. Miller, "The Least Orthodox Reading is to be Preferred: A New Canon for New Testament Textual Criticism?" in Wallace, ed., *Revisiting the Corruption of the New Testament,* 57–89.

9. Ibid., 245.

10. H. Wayne House and Joseph M. Holden, *Charts of Apologetics and Christian Evidences* (Grand Rapids: Zondervan, 2006), 40.

11. Ibid., 42.

12. Tertullian wrote about A.D. 180, "Come now, you who would indulge a better curiosity, if you would apply it to the business of your salvation, run over [to] the apostolic churches, in which the very thrones of the apostles are still pre-eminent in their places, in which their own authentic writings are read, uttering the voice and representing the face of each of them severally." *De Praescriptione Haereticorum,* ch. 36, Schaff's translation. The *Oxford Latin Dictionary* and Lewis and Short's *A Latin Dictionary* translate the Latin word *authenticus* as "original writing," or autographs. Since Tertullian focuses on the different churches that initially received the apostolic writings, it is likely that he considered the autographs

in his days to be still housed at these churches. See Daniel B. Wallace, "Did the Original New Testament Manuscripts Still Exist in the Second Century?," http://www.bible.org/article /did-original-new-testament-manuscripts-still-exist-second -century#P8_648.

Part 8: The Translation of the Bible

1. Randall Price, *Searching for the Original Bible* (Eugene, OR: Harvest House, 2007), 59.
2. Paul D. Wegner, *The Journey from Texts to Translations: The Origin and Development of the Bible* (Grand Rapids: Baker, 1999), 173–74.
3. Price, *Searching for the Original Bible*, 58.
4. Ibid., 59–60. For a more complete description of these texts and others, and for a more extensive description of the Masoretic Text, see Ernst Würthwein, *The Text of the Old Testament*, 2nd ed., trans. Erroll F. Rhodes (Grand Rapids: Eerdmans, 1995), 35–38 and 10–44 respectively.
5. Leland Ryken, *Choosing a Bible: Understanding Bible Translation Differences* (Wheaton, IL: Crossway, 2005), 6.
6. Ibid.
7. Ibid., 7.
8. Ibid., 13–14.
9. Ibid., 18–19.
10. For an excellent and readable overview of the various translations and versions available, see Ron Rhodes, *The Complete Guide to Bible Translations* (Eugene, OR: Harvest House, 2009).

    For a more in-depth study of the translation theories and how they affect English Bible translations, see Leland Ryken, *The Word of God in English: Criteria for Excellence in Bible Translation* (Wheaton, IL: Crossway, 2002).
11. See Ryken, *The Word of God in English*, for an excellent treatment of Bible translation by a professor of comparative literature at Wheaton College.

12. Ryken, *The Word of God in English*, 287–93.
13. For a thorough primer to the Septuagint, see Karen H. Jobes and Moisés Silva, *Invitation to the Septuagint* (Grand Rapids: Baker, 2000).
14. Ibid., 23.
15. Wegner, *Journey from Texts to Translations*, 195.
16. Ibid.
17. Jobes and Silva, *Invitation to the Septuagint*, 20.
18. Ibid., 26.
19. Wegner, *Journey from Texts to Translations*, 252–53. See also Würthwein, *Text of the Old Testament*, 91–92.
20. Würthwein, *Text of the Old Testament*, 96.
21. Wegner, *Journey from Texts to Translations*, 256.
22. Würthwein, *Text of the Old Testament*, 98.
23. Ibid.
24. Ibid., 85.
25. Ibid., 86.
26. Wegner, *Journey from Texts to Translations*, 202.
27. Ibid., 203.
28. Ibid., 202.
29. Price, *Searching for the Original Bible*, 71–74.
30. Würthwein, *Text of the Old Testament*, 46.
31. For an overview of the Samaritan Pentateuch, see Bruce K. Waltke, "Samaritan Pentateuch," in *Anchor Bible Dictionary,* ed. David Noel Freedman, 6 vols. (New York: Doubleday, 1992), 5:932–40.

Part 9: The Interpretation of the Bible

1. The following questions on interpretation of the Bible are based on, and adapted from, sections on biblical interpretation found in *The House Visual Study Bible* (Olive Tree Bible Software) and *How to Interpret the Bible by What It Says* (Olive Tree Bible Software). The graphics are also from these works.

2. Milton S. Terry, *Biblical Hermeneutics* (Grand Rapids: Zondervan, n.d.), 205.

3. H. Wayne House, "The Difference Between Meaning and Interpretation," http://www.hwhouse.com/publications/charts.html; © 2001 H. Wayne House. All rights reserved.

4. H. Wayne House, "The Difference Between Meaning and Implication," http://www.hwhouse.com/publications/charts.html; © 2001 H. Wayne House. All rights reserved.

5. H. Wayne House, "The Distinction Between Literal and Figurative Language in Determining Literal Truth," http://www.hwhouse.com/publications/charts.html; © 2011 H. Wayne House. All rights reserved.

6. H. Wayne House, "The Process of Interpretation," http://www.hwhouse.com/publications/charts.html; © 2001 H. Wayne House. All rights reserved.

Part 10: Contemporary Challenges Regarding the Bible

1. H. Wayne House and Timothy J. Demy, "Non-Canonical Sources Referred to by Paul and Jude in the New Testament," http://www.hwhouse.com/publications/charts.html; © 2011 H. Wayne House and Timothy J. Demy. All rights reserved. 1 Enoch translation from George W. E. Nicklelsburg and James C. VanderKam, *1 Enoch: A New Translation* (Minneapolis: Fortress, 2004), 20.

2. For a good overview of the Dead Sea Scrolls, see Allen Ross, "The Witness of the Dead Sea Scrolls," Bible.org, http://www.bible.org/seriespage/witness-dead-sea-scrolls. For two very readable studies of the Dead Sea Scrolls that provide ample information on their relation to the Bible, see Randall Price, *Secrets of the Dead Sea Scrolls* (Eugene, OR: Harvest House, 1995); and Craig A. Evans, *Holman QuickSource Guide to the Dead Sea Scrolls* (Nashville: B&H, 2010).

3. Evans, *Holman QuickSource Guide to the Dead Sea Scrolls*, 44–45.

4. Ibid., 46–48.

5. Daniel B. Wallace, "7Q5: The Earliest NT Papyrus?," Bible .org, http://www.bible.org/article/7q5=earliest-nt-papyrus. See also Evans, *Holman QuickSource Guide to the Dead Sea Scrolls*, 369–72.

6. Cited in Evans, *Holman QuickSource Guide to the Dead Sea Scrolls*, 311.

7. Ibid., 324–25. See pp. 327–68 for a deeper comparison of the scrolls and the New Testament.

8. Ibid., 381.

9. See John Farrell, "Fragments of Mark's Gospel May Date to 1st Century," *Forbes Online,* February 27, 2012, at http://www .forbes.com/sites/johnfarrell/2012/02/27/fragments-of-marks -gospel-may-date-to-1st-century/. To follow this and other developments in New Testament textual studies, see Dan Wallace's blog at http://www.danielbwallace.com.

10. F. F. Bruce, *The New Testament Documents: Are They Reliable?* (Grand Rapids: Eerdmans, 1960), 15.

11. Wayne House and Timothy J. Demy, "Comparison of Manuscripts of Ancient Literature and the New Testament, http://www.hwhouse.com/publications/charts.html; © 2001 H. Wayne House and Timothy J. Demy. All rights reserved.

Conclusion

1. Carl F. H. Henry, *Carl Henry at His Best: A Lifetime of Quotable Thoughts* (Portland, OR: WaterBrook Multnomah, 1989), 28.

Recommended Reading

Ankerberg, John, and John Weldon. *The Facts on the King James Only Debate*. Eugene, OR: Harvest House, 1996.

Archer, Gleason L., and G. C. Chirichigno, *Old Testament Quotations in the New Testament: A Complete Survey*. Chicago: Moody Press, 1983.

Bauckham, Richard. *Jesus and the Eyewitnesses: The Gospel as Eyewitness Testimony*. Grand Rapids: Eerdmans, 2006.

Berding, Kenneth, and Jonathan Lunde, eds. *Three Views on the New Testament Use of the Old Testament*. Grand Rapids: Zondervan, 2008.

Black, David Alan, ed. *Perspectives on the Ending of Mark: Four Views*. Nashville: B&H, 2008.

Bock, Darrell L. *Breaking the Da Vinci Code*. Nashville: Thomas Nelson, 2004.

_____. *The Missing Gospels: Unearthing the Truth Behind Alternative Christianities*. Nashville: Thomas Nelson, 2006.

_____. *Recovering the Real Lost Gospel: Reclaiming the Gospel as Good News*. Nashville: B&H, 2010.

Bock, Darrell L., and Daniel B. Wallace. *Dethroning Jesus: Exposing Popular Culture's Quest to Unseat the Biblical Christ*. Nashville: Thomas Nelson, 2007.

Bruce, F. F. *The Canon of Scripture*. Westmont, IL: InterVarsity, 1988.

_____. *The New Testament Documents: Are They Reliable?* Grand Rapids: Eerdmans, 1960.

Comfort, Philip W. *The Complete Guide to Bible Versions.* Wheaton,
    IL: Tyndale House, 1991.

_____. *New Testament Text and Translation Commentary.* Whea-
    ton, IL: Tyndale House, 2008.

Comfort, Philip W., ed. *The Origin of the Bible.* Wheaton, IL: Tyn-
    dale House, 1992.

Demy, Tim, and Gary Stewart. *101 Most Puzzling Bible Verses.*
    Eugene, OR: Harvest House, 2006.

Evans, Craig A. *Holman QuickSource Guide to the Dead Sea Scrolls.*
    Nashville: B&H, 2010.

_____. *Noncanonical Writings and New Testament Interpretation.*
    Peabody, MA: Hendrickson, 1992.

Fouts, David M. "A Defense of the Hyperbolic Interpretation of
    Large Numbers in the Old Testament." *Journal of the Evan-
    gelical Theological Society* 40, no. 3 (1997): 377–87.

_____. "The Incredible Numbers of the Hebrew Kings." In *Giv-
    ing the Sense: Understanding and Using Old Testament His-
    torical Texts,* edited by David M. Howard Jr. and Michael A.
    Grisanti, 283–99. Grand Rapids: Kregel, 2003.

Freedman, David Noel. "The Earliest Bible." In *Backgrounds for the
    Bible,* edited by Michael Patrick O'Connor and David Noel
    Freedman, 29–38. Winona Lake, IN: Eisenbrauns, 1987.

Geisler, Norman L., ed. *Inerrancy.* Grand Rapids: Zondervan, 1980.

Geisler, Norman L., and William E. Nix. *From God to Us: How We
    Got Our Bible.* Chicago: Moody Press, 1974.

_____. *A General Introduction to the Bible,* rev. ed. Chicago:
    Moody Press, 1986.

Gerhardsson, Birger. *Memory and Manuscript with Tradition and
    Transmission in Early Christianity.* Grand Rapids: Eerd-
    mans, 1998.

Hannam, James. *The Genesis of Science: How the Late Christian Mid-
    dle Ages Launched the Scientific Revolution.* Washington,
    D.C.: Regnery, 2011.

_____. *God's Philosophers: How the Medieval World Laid the Foundations of Modern Science.* London: Icon, 2010.

Hemer, Colin J. *The Book of Acts in the Setting of Hellenistic History.* Edited by Conrad H. Gempf. Winona Lake, IN: Eisenbrauns, 1990.

Henry, Carl F. H. *God, Revelation and Authority.* 6 vols. Waco: Word, 1976–83.

House, H. Wayne. *Chronological and Background Charts of the New Testament.* 2nd ed. Grand Rapids: Zondervan, 2009.

House, H. Wayne, ed. *Intelligent Design 101: Leading Experts Explain the Key Issues.* Grand Rapids: Kregel, 2008.

House, H. Wayne, and Joseph M. Holden. *Charts of Apologetics and Christian Evidences.* Grand Rapids: Zondervan, 2006.

House, H. Wayne, and Dennis W. Jowers. *Reasons for Our Hope: An Introduction to Christian Apologetics.* Nashville: B&H, 2011.

Jobes, Karen H., and Moisés Silva. *Invitation to the Septuagint.* Grand Rapids: Baker, 2000.

Jones, Timothy Paul. *Misquoting Truth: A Guide to the Fallacies of Bart Ehrman's Misquoting Jesus.* Westmont, IL: InterVarsity, 2007.

Kaiser, Walter, C. Jr. *The Old Testament Documents: Are They Reliable and Relevant?* Westmont, IL: InterVarsity, 2001.

Kitchen, K. A. *On the Reliability of the Old Testament.* Grand Rapids: Eerdmans, 2003.

Longenecker, Richard N. *Biblical Exegesis in the Apostolic Period.* 2nd ed. Grand Rapids: Eerdmans, 1999.

McDowell, Josh. *The New Evidence That Demands a Verdict.* Nashville: Thomas Nelson, 1999.

Metzger, Bruce M. "The Apocrypha and Pseudepigrapha." In *The Expositor's Bible Commentary.* Vol. 1, *Introductory Articles.* Edited by Frank E. Gaebelein, 161–74. Grand Rapids: Zondervan, 1979.

_____. *The Canon of the New Testament: Its Origin, Development, and Significance.* Oxford: Oxford University Press, 1987.

_____. "Important Early Translations of the Bible," *Bibliotheca Sacra* 150, no. 597 (1993): 35–49.

_____. *An Introduction to the Apocrypha*. New York: Oxford University Press, 1957.

_____. *The Text of the New Testament: Its Transmission, Corruption, and Restoration*. 3rd ed. New York: Oxford University Press, 1992.

Patzia, Arthur G. *The Making of the New Testament: Origin, Collection, Text and Canon*. 2nd ed. Westmont, IL: InterVarsity, 2011.

Plummer, Robert L. *40 Questions About Interpreting the Bible*. Grand Rapids: Kregel, 2010.

Price, Randall. *Searching for the Original Bible*. Eugene, OR: Harvest House, 2007.

_____. *Secrets of the Dead Sea Scrolls*. Eugene, OR: Harvest House, 1995.

Rhodes, Ron. *The Complete Guide to Bible Translations*. Eugene, OR: Harvest House, 2009.

Roberts, Mark D. *Can We Trust the Gospels? Investigating the Reliability of Matthew, Mark, Luke, and John*. Wheaton, IL: Crossway, 2007.

Ross, Allen. "The Witness of the Dead Sea Scrolls." Bible.org. http://www.bible.org/seriespage/witness-dead-sea-scrolls.

Ryken, Leland. *Choosing a Bible: Understanding Bible Translation Differences*. Wheaton, IL: Crossway, 2005.

_____. *The Word of God in English: Criteria for Excellence in Bible Translation*. Wheaton, IL: Crossway, 2002.

Ryrie, Charles C. *Basic Theology*. Colorado Springs: Victor, 1982.

_____. *What You Should Know about Inerrancy*. Chicago: Moody Press, 1981.

Shanks, Hershel. "When Did Ancient Israel Begin?" *Biblical Archaeology Review* 38, no. 1 (2012): 59–62, 67.

Wallace, Daniel B. "Did the Original New Testament Manuscripts Still Exist in the Second Century?" Bible.org. http://bible.org

/article/did-original-new-testament-manuscripts-still
-exist-second-century-0.

Wallace, Daniel B., ed. *Revisiting the Corruption of the New Testament: Manuscript, Patristic, and Apocryphal Evidence.* Grand Rapids: Kregel, 2011.

Waltke, Bruce K. "Aims of OT Textual Criticism." *Westminster Theological Journal* 51, no. 1 (1989): 93–108.

————. "Samaritan Pentateuch." In *Anchor Bible Dictionary*, edited by David Noel Freedman 5:932–40. New York: Doubleday, 1992.

Wegner, Paul D. *The Journey from Texts to Translations: The Origin and Development of the Bible.* Grand Rapids: Baker, 2000.

White, James R. *The King James Only Controversy.* Minneapolis: Bethany House, 1995.

Würthwein, Ernst. *The Text of the Old Testament.* 2nd ed. Translated by Erroll F. Rhodes. Grand Rapids: Eerdmans, 1995.

Young, B. H. "Targum." In *The International Standard Bible Encyclopedia*, edited by Geoffrey W. Bromiley 4:727–33. Grand Rapids: Eerdmans, 1988.

Zuck, Roy B. *Basic Bible Interpretation: A Practical Guide to Discovering Biblical Truth.* Colorado Springs: Victor, 1991.

About the Authors

H. Wayne House is distinguished research professor of theology, law, and culture at Faith Evangelical Seminary in Tacoma, Washington, and an adjunct professor of biblical studies and apologetics at Veritas Evangelical Seminary. Formerly he was associate professor of systematic theology at Dallas Theological Seminary; professor of theology and culture at Trinity Graduate School, Trinity International University; and professor of law at Trinity Law School. He has a JD from Regent University School of Law; a ThD from Concordia Seminary, St. Louis; an MA in Patristic Greek from Abilene Christian University; a ThM and MDiv from Western Seminary; and a BA in Classical and Hellenistic Greek from Hardin-Simmons University.

He has been the author, coauthor, and editor of over thirty books, the author of more than seventy journal and magazine publications, and a contributor to several books, dictionaries, and encyclopedias. Among his many books are *The Nelson Study Bible* (NT editor); *The Battle for God*; *Charts on Open Theism and Orthodoxy*; *Charts of World Religions*; *Charts of Christian Theology and Doctrine*; *Chronological and Background Charts of the New Testament*; *Charts of Cults, Sects, and Religious Movements*; *A Christian View of Law*; *Restoring the Constitution*; *The Jesus Who Never Lived*; *Israel: The Land and the People*; *God's Message: Your Sermon*; and *Intelligent Design 101*.

Dr. House serves on the board of numerous organizations and served as president of the Evangelical Theological Society (1991).

He leads study tours to Israel every year, and on alternate years to Jordan and Egypt, and Turkey and Greece. He has been married to Leta Frances McConnell for forty-five years and they have two grown children, Carrie and Nathan, and five grandchildren. He may be contacted at info@christianstudytours.com for interest in travel to biblical lands. His website is www.hwhouse.com.

Timothy J. Demy has authored and edited more than two dozen books on the Bible, theology, and current issues. He has also contributed to numerous journals, Bible handbooks, study Bibles, and theological encyclopedias. Among his books are *War, Peace, and Christianity: Questions and Answers from a Just-War Perspective; 101 Most Puzzling Bible Verses, Answers to Common Questions about Angels and Demons; Answers to Common Questions about Heaven and Eternity; Answers to Common Questions about Jesus; and Answers to Common Questions about the End Times.* A professor of military ethics at the U.S. Naval War College, he served more than twenty-seven years as a military chaplain in a variety of assignments afloat and ashore with the U.S. Navy, U.S. Marine Corps, and U.S. Coast Guard. He has published and spoken nationally and internationally on issues of war and peace and the role of religion in international relations. He also serves as an adjunct professor of theology at Baptist Bible Seminary in Clarks Summit, Pennsylvania.

In addition to his theological training, which he received at Dallas Theological Seminary (ThM, ThD), he received the MSt in international relations from the University of Cambridge and MA and PhD degrees from Salve Regina University, where he wrote about C. S. Lewis. He also earned graduate degrees in European history and in national security and strategic studies and was the President's Honor Graduate from the U.S. Naval War College. He is a member of numerous professional organizations, including the Evangelical Theological Society and the Society of Biblical Literature, and is a fellow of the Royal Society of Arts, UK. He and his wife, Lyn, have been married thirty-five years.